PRAYING
WITH THE NEW
CATECHISM

MICHAEL HOLLINGS

PRAYING
WITH THE NEW
CATECHISM

INCLUDES SECTION FOUR OF THE CATECHISM
CHRISTIAN PRAYER

McCRIMMONS
Great Wakering Essex

First published in Great Britain by MCCRIMMON PUBLISHING CO LTD
10–12 High Street, Great Wakering, Essex SS3 0EQ
Tel: (01702) 218956 Fax: (01702) 216082

Commentary on Praying with the New Catechism
© 1994 Michael Hollings

ISBN 0 85597 539 3

Cover design by Nick Snode
Typeset in 11.5pt New Baskerville and 11pt Sabon by McCrimmons

Reprographics by Anagram Litho Ltd, Southend–on–sea
Printed on 80gsm white bond
Printed by Black Bear Press Ltd, Cambridge

CONTENTS

CHRISTIAN PRAYER
A COMMENTARY BY MICHAEL HOLLINGS

I came to the study of this part of the New Catechism with some trepidation, because I did not know what to expect. Having given all the time I could to it, I want to say that reading, praying and studying the text have been spiritually very valuable for me personally. I therefore conclude that anyone who makes the space to absorb the contents will also benefit greatly.

In general, the presentation and style are direct and simple. The language is straightforward and not obscure. It is easy to read and easy to understand.

Although the whole Catechism will be widely circulated and no doubt widely studied and read, it is a solid and perhaps intimidating volume for many ordinary people. My fear would be that while the vast majority of all ages will hear of it and have some talk about it from the pulpit, school or college, they will never become properly familiar with the content. In course of time there will no doubt be a successor to the 'penny catechism', but the penny catechism, admirable as it was, would be too condensed a form to unfold the richness of this particular section, Book Four, on Prayer. I suggested that thought be given to making this section available, as soon as possible, on its own and this book is the result.

Book Four is sub-divided into two parts, three chapters and various articles, which I will cover as we go along. Part One is Prayer in the 'Christian Life' (2558–2758). Part Two is an extended exposition of The Lord's Prayer – Our Father (2759–2865).

PART ONE
Prayer in the Christian Life

What is Prayer?

Like many older people, I was brought up on the simple catechism definition of prayer, 'The raising of the mind and heart to God'. This was adequate to me at first, but experience showed that people seemed to put the stress on the mind rather to the neglect of the heart: 'Prayer is ascent of the mind to God or the

7

request of blessing from God'.[1] Now, in theory and practice there is a wider sense of the mystery of faith being lived out in personal, conscious and responsible relationship with the living and true God. There is better balance here: 'For me, prayer means launching out of the heart towards God; it means lifting up one's eyes, quite simply, to heaven, a cry of grateful love, from the crest of joy or the trough of despair'.[2]

This is a broader approach and takes us back into the tradition of Scripture, where the heart is most strongly stated as the source of prayer. The re-discovery of the heart is much at the centre of prayer in recent times. These first few pages set the tone for the rest of the exposition of prayer – living relationship, covenant, presence of God, communion of the whole person with God. We have not always recognised or accepted that we have much in common in prayer with other faiths and that we have learnt and can learn from them. However, we need to remember the significant distinction that Christian prayer is a communion with Christ individually and it also embraces his body the Church, extending as far as Christ's own love (2565).

2566 ## The Revelation of Prayer

The universal call to prayer is set in the history of humanity from creation. This reminds us that we do not just begin with the revelation of God in Jesus Christ. It is a useful perspective because it links us into the history of humanity, drawing out for us God's call as seen through individuals, tribes and centuries before Christ.

2568 *The Old Testament.* This is a creative passage in which the various aspects of prayer are brought into focus through key figures of the bible story. Stress is laid on the virtue of prayer being lived by 'many righteous people of all religions'.

2569 To me, the covenant with Noah is so important. It is made with 'every living creature' and it is signalised by the 'arc in the sky', the rainbow. We all know that the rainbow comes into being by the mingling of the rays of the sun and the falling rain. We do not always realise the meaning of this in our lives – lives which themselves create a rainbow as we experience joys and

---

1 St John Damascene, *De Fide Orth, 3.24: PG94, 1089c*
2 *St Thérèse of Lisieux. The Autobiography of a Saint* (tr. Ronald Knox, London, Collins 1960, 228)

sorrows, bouncing good health and illness. This pattern mirrors the variety of our prayer where eruptions of love are tempered with dryness, lethargy and even a sense of being abandoned altogether by God … the rainbow of life, the rainbow of prayer.

Abraham, Jacob, Moses and David. Abraham, held up as the great [2570–80] man of faith who is utterly obedient to God, gains his strength from the openness of his heart. He was a silent, practical person and went about what he had to do in life quietly, uncomplainingly. God tested him, as he does each of us, which is another facet of the rainbow of life. When God asks him the ultimate obedience in the gift of his son Isaac for sacrifice, we have a foretaste of God sending his own son, who in turn becomes obedient unto death, even death on the cross.

Frankly, the tale of Esau's loss at the hands of Jacob has always been more than puzzling to me. I always remember a reading in the breviary when we were informed that that Jacob's statement to his father was 'not a lie but a mystery'. However, before this lie, Jacob had had his encounter with an angel, now called a mysterious stranger.

This wrestling underlines the toughness of the life of prayer. [2574–77] Centuries ago it was called The Spiritual Combat (SCUPOLI)[3]. It is necessary for us to understand that the life of prayer does not simply happen to us, like being hungry as children and being given food by a loving parent. Rather, we have to accept that the life of prayer demands a continual effort, a regular commitment and steadfastness.

With Moses we meet the great interceder. For the ordinary person, it can be very reassuring to know that intercession is a vital and very prominent part of our common prayer. Perhaps the comforting part of Moses' intercession from our viewpoint is that he is not interceding once and getting an answer, but goes at it over and over again. The people of Israel, and we in our day, constantly tried the patience of God. Moses witnesses to this patience, and to the patience we seem often to need in relation to God, when our intercessions are not promptly answered.

David is a very different man of prayer. His legacy is a legacy of [2578–80]

---

3 *Spiritual Combat: A Treatize on Inward Peace,* by Lorenzo Scupoli (1530–1610), Theatine Father in Naples. Read daily by St. Francis de Sales.

life, left to us especially in the Psalms. These manage to cover the whole breadth, height and depth of our human predicament. After all, he personally experienced the whole gamut of possible glory and shame. He is called 'the first Prophet of Jewish and Christian prayer'. The Psalter grew from this and is here described and praised: The Psalter is the book in which God's word becomes our prayer – simple and spontaneous, full of faith – 'The Praises'.

Elijah. Elijah appears again with Moses in the New Testament at the Transfiguration of Christ. There they represent the Law and the Prophets, linking the Old and the New. Elijah also links the East of today in the Orthodox liturgies, where his pleading with God: 'Answer me, O Lord, answer me' is used in the eucharistic epiclesis. Elijah is the father of the prophets and he calls the people through faith to conversion of the heart. The whole of this section is very helpful in expounding and encouraging us to explore the richness of the Old Testament and to appreciate how the development of worship in the assembly has flowed through into our constant use of the Psalter in our daily personal prayers and Offices and liturgy.

2585–89

2598–2619

In the Fullness of Time

2599–2606 **Jesus Prays.** This article looks at Jesus himself at and in prayer – then Jesus teaching prayer. There is a simple expression here of the early hidden life of Jesus and how he learned to be human – learning to pray in his human heart, at his Mother's knee, among his people, in the synagogue and Temple, in Nazareth and Jerusalem. This is important because, knowing as little as we do about the years before the public ministry of Jesus, we can either make up pretty stories or dismiss those thirty years. Yet they represent the major part of his life on earth in the flesh and are to me an endless source of contemplation, because there are no facts to distract the mind. We, who rush so quickly into growing up and 'knowing everything', find the Son of God taking years and years doing his Father's will – perhaps in our terms wasting time. Here is a profound lesson for ourselves and for the guidance of young people.

St Luke is the most detailed and moving of the Evangelists in telling us of Jesus' prayer habits and his teaching of prayer. Among the essential points which stand out are these, each highlighted in Luke. He goes away to a quiet place; he often goes alone to pray to his Father, but he also prays in the presence of his disciples: he prays with thanksgiving; he prays at each important time in his life. He always seeks his Father's will and prays that it be done. Prayer continues to the very end, when he finally commits himself into his Father's hands.

Jesus Teaches us how to pray   2607–16

From the beginning of his teaching conversion of heart, reconciliation and love are central. As son, he teaches us to be bold and to pray with faith. He reiterates the theme of struggle, even in keeping awake and watching in prayer. Faith and love intermingle. He also assures us of the attitude of himself and his Father in listening to our prayer when we see him listening to the prayers and requests of ordinary people. We are not gods, but if we thought a bit we would see that human beings every day are receiving the prayers of other human beings, and making their own prayers not only to God but to their friends, relations, teachers, neighbours and so on. If someone asks me for a cup of tea, it is a prayer. If I answer by giving that cup of tea, it is an answer to a prayer. It also works through our actions, and hence the last judgement will be a judgement on love in prayer and action.

We can also learn from Jesus, perhaps, that the art of listening in prayer makes us better able to listen to those who pray our affection, our time, our love, our listening, our goods, our support.

The Prayer of the Virgin Mary   2617–19

At the end of this section there is a brief look at Mary's prayer. The basis – out of her heart, of her faith, her humility, her trust, her love and her very self – is her *Fiat* … 'let it be to me according to your word'.

For me, the deep import of Mary's life is her overall silence. We hear her fiat, her Magnificat, her intervention at Cana. The first teaches us the need for faith and trust in prayer and life, then the emphasis on praise, thanks and humility, in the third, the importance of intercession.

In The Age of the Church   2623–49

Here there is a glance at the infant church at and after Pentecost. It is interesting that there is stress on the forms of prayer which are mentioned in the Acts of the Apostles, which are seen as the norm for Christian prayer. The sense of dialogue between God and his creatures is strong – blessing, being blessed, receiving blessing, returning blessing.

2631   There follows a passage on adoration and petition, which contains a point which had not struck me before in this way. The statement made is that 'the first movement of the prayer of petition is asking forgiveness', instancing the parable of the tax collector and publican – Have mercy on me, a sinner. It goes on to say: 'asking forgiveness introduces both the eucharistic liturgy and personal prayer'. These lead naturally to praise and thanksgiving, seen especially in the eucharist. The tradition that the Eucharist is a sacrifice of praise and thanksgiving is common to both East and West.

Petition is seen as different in a way from intercession, but for many this is just a question of semantics. Both are asking: petition is considered more for myself, intercession for others.

2650–93

The Tradition of Prayer

2652   **The Sources of Prayer**

Quite rightly it is made clear that prayer is more than just an outpouring spontaneously of something within us. It certainly can happen now and then in the lives of any individuals. But the basis of prayer lies in our hearts and wills. It is not a matter of just knowing about Scripture or about Christ. We have to discipline ourselves to be with Christ as he is with us, and to know him is essential in order to love him more. Knowing about him, through listening to him in the Bible, reading about him, hearing others teaching or preaching about him – this is all valuable background which we need to grow in prayer. Reading and studying is excellent, but to go forward in our spiritual growth we have to pray what we are reading and studying.

2655   *The Liturgy of the Church:* The word of God is intimately connected to the Liturgy. It is regrettable that the opportunity to expound a little on the word of God at each Mass on each day is seldom taken up by the celebrant. It is also sad that generally speaking little time for silence is given. Rather than being a meditative experience of prayerful worship, the whole Mass can be almost non-stop words, either spoken or sung. The Eucharist is not always comfortable. It can be distracting, boring, patronising on the part of the priest, or just a habit to be gone through. But remember the background of liturgy and prayer are the virtues of faith, hope and charity, if we can learn to practise them.

They help us to pray with faith, to look forward in hope to the coming of God's kingdom of justice, love and peace, and to live day by day in the love of God, our neighbours – and in their service. De Caussade's 'Sacrament of the Present Moment' is most apposite, following St. Paul's injunction to pray at all times. It seems to be necessary for us to work out ways to bring ourselves back to prayer in the breaks between our busy–ness during each twenty–four hours.

2656

The Way of Prayer. Sometimes in the past, a criticism of the Catholic Church has been that undue prominence is given to praying to the Virgin Mary, at the expense of centring on Chirst. This Catechism sets the focus very firmly on Christ – there is no other way of Christian prayer than Christ. This is the straight way to God through Jesus, in the Spirit of the Father.

2663

Prayer to Jesus. Our liturgy not only centres on the sacrifice of Jesus but concentrates our prayer to him and through him. There is no way round this. And this is mirrored in all the christian liturgical traditions ... But the name of Jesus, the Holy Name, has probably been more used in the east than the west, even though some of our older devotions, now largely lost, have been an exception. The Orthodox churches in particular have had a tremendous influence over a multiplicity of souls through the Jesus Prayer. However, we ourselves have the other mystical tradition in such writings as The Cloud of Unknowing or Juliana of Norwich. The use of the name of Jesus has also become an abuse, an expletive. I will always remember a teenager who the night before he died of cancer as I was with him in hospital kept on saying: 'Jesus! Jesus!' Then he turned his head to me and said: 'I'm not swearing I'm praying'.

2665

Come Holy Spirit. In my early days, I seldom thought consciously of the Holy Spirit in my prayer. Confirmation came and went without the flutter of wings or any sense of warm inpouring. I really came across the power of the Spirit through the life and work of St Philip Neri, that great apostle of Rome, young people and the poor – and founder of the Oratory. Perhaps this

2670

was true of a wider element of the Church which has happily changed since about the 1970s. There has been a re–awakening through the Charismatic Movement and other influences, leading to a freer expression in prayer and praise, opening up prayer meetings, the laying on of hands, healing, speaking in tongues. It is not the purpose of this section to be 'charismatic', we are reminded that the Holy Spirit permeates all our prayer and being, and so must be responsible for the living tradition of prayer.

2673 *Prayer in Communion with the Holy Mother of God.* The end of this section goes a little further than the earlier mention of Mary. It re–emphasises her original commitment and then her continued fidelity to her promise. Jesus came into the world to do his Father's will; Mary is seen as his sign to show us his way of faith and love.

The phrases of the Hail Mary are examined one by one. This causes me to comment how necessary it is that parents and teachers should teach children the basic prayers like Our Father and Hail Mary. Sadly, I have found in visiting Catholic homes and also Catholic schools that there seems to be a large number of children who do not even know the Hail Mary. In our local primary school, we have set up a programme of prayers to be learned and prayed year by year. I'm afraid there is little evidence of families praying together; the family rosary, which admittedly had its problems, has virtually disappeared. However, there has been a welcome growth in rosary groups in many different areas. Perhaps this is partly because a number of priests and teachers have given up the devotion.

2683 *Guides for Prayer.* The theme of the family being the first place of education in prayer continues under this title. There is an atmosphere of the communion of saints, going right back to the time of the prophets and those who received their spirit to hand on to others. Christianity is not alone in singling out the family as foundational for the formation of husband and wife together, who in their turn give their spirit on to their children. Often we may be tempted to think that only specially trained counsellors or spiritual directors, clergy or sisters can help others to pray. But down the ages there have been, as there are today, prayerful, wise and holy people who are well able through their own experience to share with and assist others on their inward journey. They should be prepared for marriage, with some teaching about their responsibility when bearing children. This hopefully is reinforced in Baptism preparation, when their child is entrusted to them as 'the first and best educators'.

A church is a house of God, a place set aside for prayer and worship. The christian home should be a family home where God is always present among us. It is an old practice in a Catholic home to have some outward sign of God's presence visible to all in the house and all visitors: a statue, a crucifix, or a picture of the Sacred Heart or Our Lady. Unhappily, the custom is not so prevalent today, though some Irish families and many from the West Indies, India or the Philippines, among those I frequently visit, still proudly and lovingly display their living faith on the walls of their living rooms. This, together with the practice of having a home blessed and dedicated to the Sacred Heart, should continue and be developed. It is good and salutary not only for the family but also for visitors. Christians should look at the prayer habits of the Hindus and Muslims. Muslims have a prayer mat which can be laid out at time of prayer, and, wherever possible, the Hindu family will have a prayer corner in the home.

The Life of Prayer   2697

Prayer is the life of the heart renewed. The re-iterated urging for prayer at all times echoes St. Paul's call: 'We must remember God more often than we breathe'.

To support this, we are reminded of the Church's tradition of daily offices. But in addition, we are reminded of well-tried customs such as morning and evening prayers, grace before and after meals and so on. Like previously mentioned 'dying' customs, these are in danger of disappearing, so it is good to see them re-stated.

Expressions of Prayer   2700

Vocal prayer. St John of the Cross wrote somewhere that no two souls go more than half way on the same path to God. This freedom and variety are at the heart of our human individuality and an essential part of personal prayer.

However, the text underlines of the three major expressions of prayer – vocal prayer, meditation and contemplation – and then looks at each.

Jesus himself told us not to use many words, but vocal prayer probably has always been and remains the first and lasting way of prayer. In practice, we were given the Our Father by Jesus, and the Hail Mary has biblical foundation. More generally, in the modern idiom, it is suggested to young people and others that they should express themselves to God in their own words.

I always think it is worth remembering that Scripture tells us that Jesus himself was using vocal prayer in the Garden of Gethsemani and even on the Cross at his last breath – *It is finished.*

Over the years of my priesthood, visiting uncounted numbers of death beds, I have often seen that the last conscious act of a dying person has been a gesture or word of prayer. Vocal prayer is not a gabble! The penny Catechism used to tell us: Those who think neither of God nor of what they say, do not pray well. This remains true.

2705–24   *Meditation and Mental Prayer*. It may seem like a matter of semantics, the difference in meaning between meditation and mental prayer.

'Meditation is above all a quest', so says the text. The danger over the centuries is that the word 'meditation' has tended in teaching and practice to be associated solely with the use of the mind and imagination. This meant that too frequently it was more a cerebral and imagination exercise than an engagement of love, whereas it should lead to the involvement of the heart.

2705–08   *Meditation*. It is acknowledged that there is a great variety of methods of meditation, but here they are barely touched on. But in the post-conciliar period new life has been breathed into the term 'meditation'. In the past, Ignatian meditation tended to become somewhat dry and with too little involvement of the heart. My impression is that in the past say fifteen years, the true, deep and rich legacy of St Ignatius himself has been rediscovered and found a wide and deep acceptance and practice thoughout the world.

Another form of meditation goes right back to the Desert Fathers and links closely not only with Eastern Christian practice, but also with the gurus of Asia; this is the use of the 'mantra', of sitting upright in silence, in using breathing techniques. The 'Mantra' is a word or phrase taken by a person or advised by a director or guru – Maranatha, Jesus, Love, Peace, My Lord and My God, Lord that I may see.

Starting in the 1960s there was a wave of interest and engagement in transcendental meditation, and the teachings of various Asian gurus recieved much publicity and a considerable following. One of those who first learned meditation from a guru was John Main, who sat beside one in Malaysia and subsequently, as a Benedictine, united what he had practised and learnt with the teachings of such masters as John Cassian. The John Main teaching which has spread very widely uses the mantra to still and form an anchor for the mind, so that the whole person can respond in depth, silence, waiting and love.

Most methods of meditation have aids to concentration and stilling – position of the body, hands, open, regular breathing and so on.

Mental Prayer. What I have described under meditation might seem to be little different from mental prayer. This thought is worth studying and praying about so that we do not limit ourselves or others in the longest journey of all – the inward journey to the centre of our own being and to the being of God. | 2709

The Struggle of Prayer. The struggle in prayer has already been touched upon. We look at it again now. I am very conscious of a beautiful print on my wall of Jacob struggling with the angel. | 2725

Objections to Prayer. We really come back to the opening question: What is prayer? It is rather easy to get varied and sometimes bizarre notions of what prayer is, what prayer yields up and what prayer demands. Normally, prayer is not easy as a long term undertaking in relationship, any more than any lasting relationship in our human world can swim along without any troubled waters. Normally there is no immediate wafting up to cloud nine, though this can happen now and then. On the whole, we take up our cross each day, we toil and sweat, are bored and weary, try to be faithful, are blank and seemingly without faith ... this is the warp and woof of prayer life. | 2726–28

Perseverance in prayer and generosity are ingredients which can make our prayer valid and growthful. As the world is full of distraction and temptation, many reasons are put forward for dropping what many see as a waste of time. Indeed, the individual involved in the struggle may well lose heart and feel it is all a waste of time.

2729-33   *Difficulties in Prayer*. It is fairly easy to make a list of difficulties in prayer. I suppose the basic one, which has to be tackled and fought out not only every day, but every hour of the day, is to decide our priorities. If we do not fix firmly on prayer as the most important priority, we shall always be distracted in prayer; other temptations, attractions, duties and so on will rise before our minds and in our hearts, when we should be centred on and in God and his love. Apathy and sloth are generally not far away. Disbelief or doubt hangs in. We can be in turmoil or drought, when we should be tranquil, at peace. Some of the text here is a bit trite.

2735-37   *Unanswered prayer*. Each person will know the difficulty when continued prayer apparently produces no response from God, and very many people will have heard others complaining that God is not listening.

    Perhaps the first and greatest lesson in prayer is patience. It is God's time, not ours, which forms the economy of prayer, petition or intercession. The second is that we should always pray 'Thy will be done'. This is not easy, because we know what we want, we may well think we know what is best for us or others. The long term attitude is to continue in prayer in faith, hope, trust and love.

2738-45   *How is prayer efficacious?* Prayer is part of God's plan for us and for the world. In praying, we are cooperating with his purpose for us and becoming co-workers, and may be sufferers with Christ in building up the body of Christ. As Christ is always with us, we can and should pray wherever we are. And this prayer is to be persevering, humble and trusting. Prayer and Christian life are inseperable.

2746-51   *Jesus' Prayer at his Final Hour*. This longest of all the prayers of Jesus we have received remains with us to read, pray and use in the liturgy. It is called the 'priestly prayer', and is linked closely to his sacrifice. It is a remarkable overview of Christ, the world, his Father's will, the prayer for the unity of creation. It is Christ's Amen and the foretaste of his Alleluia.

PART TWO
The Lord's Prayer, 'Our Father'
(2759–2855)

I have been told a very special insight into this last part of Book Four on Prayer. The author of this section is a priest of Lebanon. He wrote his meditation on the Our Father from the midst of the shelling and mortar attacks, the bombs and destruction of the capital, Beirut. The depth, thoughtfulness and serenity is in marked contrast to what I have witnessed of his surroundings.

The text chosen for the exposition of the Our Father is St Matthew's with the seven petitions (St Luke has only five). It also retains the older wording with 'art', 'thou', 'thy' and so on. At the beginning, attention is drawn to the early liturgical usage of the doxology. We mention this again later.

The Summary of the Whole Gospel

2761

Tertullian wrote that the Lord's Prayer 'is truly the summary of the whole Gospel – and since everyone has petitions which are peculiar to the circumstances of each, the regular and appropriate prayer is said first, as the foundation of further desires'.

I. *At the centre of the Scriptures*. We have already talked of the Psalms as permeating Christian prayer. St Augustine says: 'Glance through all the words of the holy prayers (in Scripture), and I do not think that you will be able to find anything in them that is not contained in the Lord's Prayer'. The whole Scripture is fulfilled in Christ.

2762

St. Thomas Aquinas wrote: 'The Lord's Prayer is the most perfect of prayers ... In it not only do we ask for everything we can desire with justice, but even for the order wherein it is suitable to desire it, so that this prayer not only teaches us to ask, but also informs our whole affectivity'. In the Lord's Prayer is contained the whole life teaching of the Sermon on the Mount.

II. *The Prayer of the Lord*. The title 'The Lord's Prayer' is given because Jesus taught and gave this prayer to his Father in heaven – a name to be shared by us. In the Gospel we hear often that Jesus prayed to his Father. As a human being he knew our needs

2765–66

as his own. He shared with us in all things except sin. He both gives us the example of praying and also teaches us to pray. For us, this prayer is stimulated and made possible by God's gift of the Holy Spirit, for the Father: 'sent the Spirit of his son into our hearts, crying, "Abba, Father!" '

2767-72   III. *The Prayer of the Church*. The early Christian Community used the Lord's Prayer three times a day in place of the eighteen benedictions of Judaism. Though we often use the Our Father as our own personal prayer, the very word 'our' widens the whole thought. The Lord teaches us to make a prayer in common for all our brothers and sisters. For he did not say 'my Father who art in heaven', but 'our' Father, offering petitions, for the common Body'. The liturgical use runs through all traditions. This is most clear in the three sacraments – Baptism, Confirmation and Eucharist. Baptism and Confirmation are special, once–in–a–lifetime graces. But we see the enshrining of the Our Father every time we share in the Eucharist: 'Placed between the eucharistic prayer (anaphora) and the communion, the Lord's Prayer sums up on the one hand all the petitions and intercessions expressed in the movement of invocation (epiclesis), and, on the other, seeks admittance to the feast of the kingdom which sacramental communion anticipates'.

2777-2801 **Our Father who art in Heaven**

2777-8   I. *We dare to say*. In our Roman liturgy, we have a selection of alternative introductions to the Lord's Prayer, of which this is one. (It might be said that in the greater spirit of freedom in the liturgy, many priests now make up their own phrases at this point, as they feel it appropriate for the day or feast etc.)

.   I often ponder on the distance we have come from the time of Jesus Christ's Israel. At that time, the name of God was too holy to be uttered. For Jesus to refer to God as Father, and then to extend that name to us for us to share was more than startling. Today, we have no sense of privilege in using 'Father'; indeed there is little awe or respect about at all. We can be too quickly familiar!

In a way, every time we say 'Our Father' we should have a great sense of love and humility, thanking God for the privilege of being his children, thanking even before we begin the prayer. Our attitude should be simple, trusting, sure of our acceptance in love by the one we dare to call Our Father!

II. *Father*. Sadly, for some people the experience of 'Father' is 2779–85
frightening, a figure who abuses, or deserts. Recently, in a girls'
school, in a class of 12+ girls, I was asked to answer questions.
The most difficult was forgiveness. I found that no less than
three out of the class of twenty had fathers who had left the
mothers, the family and the home. These girls could not understand how they could ever forgive their fathers.

But our text is rather severe on this. We are told: 'We must
purify our hearts of false paternal or maternal images, stemming from our personal and cultural history, and influencing
our relationship with God. Our Father transcends the categories of the created world; ideas derived from experience in this
world if ascribed to him may create idols to worship or if they
distort our knowledge of the true God, idols to destroy. To pray
to the Father is to enter into his mystery as he is and as the Son
has revealed him to us'. Unfortunately, in reality, it can be very
difficult to get people who have suffered across the psychological barrier from human to divine. We can only try, realising the
importance of the leap, but being gentle and patient with trou-
bled individuals.

The revelation Jesus gives comes from Jesus to us through
his Spirit. The reality has to be experienced – it hardly goes
into words. We are reborn by baptism, and become adopted
children. However, we move beyond that being incorporated
into his body, and we are made 'other Christs' through the
anointing in the Spirit.

Adoption is not a very well received term these days though
it is used strongly here. I am not sure that 'adoption' is a good
concept for today.

III. *'Our' Father*. Sometimes there is confusion about the unity 2786–93
and trinity of God. When we address the Father, we are not
separating him from the Son and the Spirit. Rather we are being united together as a large family, centring on the Father
with the Son and through the Spirit. Naturally, this prayer extends into the word of Christ in his prayer for unity. We become, in our entering the Lord's prayer, workers and prayers
for the unity for which Christ prayed.

IV. *Who art in heaven*. Heaven is not to be understood as a place 2797–2802
or space. It is a way of being. So we are not really 'looking up
there' when we raise minds and hearts and eyes 'to heaven'.

21

Rather, we should accept that God is with us ... the kingdom of God is within you.

God desires us to be living always in his presence, living in the covenant of his love, waiting on God in faith and love until the eternal and infinite love which supports us now on earth will be translated into his enfolding love and glory in eternity, in heaven.

2803–2865 The Seven Petitions

Over the centuries, much has been written on and about the Lord's Prayer: Our Father. Looking back, I remember how much I gained when I first came across St Teresa of Avila's exposition, and I have always liked to go back to it again and again.

Here we have a new meditation, taking each of the petitions in turn. It is a sensitive and deeply thought meditation. It needs to be thought and prayed by the reader, if possible, as deeply as the writer. It should not be rushed. It is an excellent source for extended meditation. I am not going to go through the seven petitions in detail, because they stand in their own right. There is really not much comment to give, which is not to say that these pieces are not worthwhile. They are, and I have much appreciated them as you will see. To do justice to them you must read them yourself, slowly, prayerfully.

2804–06   The division of the prayer, after the address to Our Father is in two parts – three petitions in the first part, four in the second part. Jesus' first concern, and the concern he passed on to his followers, is his Father.

2807   It is beautiful to be able to praise the Lord and much of prayer should be centred on praise. Before we come to ask for ourselves, Jesus teaches us to open mind and heart in praise. This is very normal in charismatic prayer; it is probably more apparent in churches other than Roman Catholic, although we have become better in some ways in more recent years. This praise is based on our faith.

2816   Based on hope is the next petition – looking forward to the great promise of the Kingdom. We would love it here and now, but its fullness will only be in the future and so we pray.

Jesus came to do the will of his Father; his Father's will is love. Jesus came to help us to the joy of doing his Fathers will, keeping the commandments, and teaching others to do the same.

Faith, hope and love – relationship to the Father through the Son and in the holy Spirit.

2822

The remaining petitions express the trust we have that our needs will be fulfilled though all the struggle we have to live in a healed way, and to win the battle against self. St Ignatius says somewhere that the battle against self is the longest in life, and that self dies half and hour after you do.

2828

In many ways, this battle is summed up in forgiveness. If our hearts are not open to forgive others, we block the flow of God's mercy. Just as we stand openly before God in the penitential rite at the beginning of the Eucharist, so we must be open to forgiving others as God forgives us; if not, if we do not play our part in the relationship of God, neighbour and self, God's forgiveness does not take root in us.

2838

Forgiveness stands at the heart of salvation: In the depth of the heart everything is bound and loosed. It is not in our power to blot out or forget an offence, but the heart that offers itself to the Holy Spirit turns injury into compassion and purifies the memory of it in transforming the hurt into prayer (2843).

The Final Doxology. It is good to find the doxology included as it has been in the Roman Catholic Liturgy since Vatican II. I can remember back to the years when we were not allowed to use the doxology, which made it very hard to join in ecumenical meetings! Of course, the Church of England uses both the shorter version and the one with the doxology; and increasingly, even outside the liturgy, I find that Roman Catholics use it as well. This is a very simple, straightforward way in which we can learn to come together.

2855

One of the moving, encouraging aspects of this Book Four on Prayer is the atmosphere it breathes of acceptance of East and West, of all God-fearing people, and reminds me of the revelation which St Peter had in the Acts of the Apostles: 'I now really understand that God has no favourites, but that anybody of any nationality who fears him and does what is right is acceptable to him'.[1]

Amen! So be it! Alleluia!

---

1   *Acts. 10.34.35*

CATECHISM
OF THE
CATHOLIC CHURCH

Part Four:
Christian Prayer

CHRISTIAN PRAYER

PART ONE

Prayer in the Christian Life

2558 'Great is the mystery of the faith!' The Church professes this mystery in the Apostles' Creed (*Part One*) and celebrates it in the sacramental liturgy (*Part Two*), so that the life of the faithful may be conformed to Christ in the Holy Spirit to the glory of God the Father (*Part Three*). This mystery, then, requires that the faithful believe in it, that they celebrate it, and that they live from it in a vital and personal relationship with the living and true God. This relationship is prayer.

What is Prayer?

For me, prayer is a surge of the heart; it is a simple look turned toward heaven, it is a cry of recognition and of love, embracing both trial and joy.[1]

Prayer as God's gift

2559 'Prayer is the raising of one's mind and heart to God or the requesting of good things from God.'[2] But when we pray, do we speak from the height of our pride and will, or 'out of the depths' of a humble and contrite heart?[3] He who humbles himself will be exalted;[4] *humility* is the foundation of prayer. Only when we humbly acknowledge that 'we do not know how to pray as we ought,'[5] are we ready to receive freely the gift of prayer. 'Man is a beggar before God.'[6]

2613
2736

2560 'If you knew the gift of God!'[7] The wonder of prayer is revealed beside the well where we come seeking water: there, Christ comes to meet every human being. It is he who first seeks us and asks us for a drink. Jesus thirsts; his asking arises from the depths of God's desire for us. Whether we realize it or not, prayer is the encounter of God's thirst with ours. God thirsts that we may thirst for him.[8]

2561 'You would have asked him, and he would have given you

---

1 St Thérèse of Lisieux, *Manuscrits autobiographiques*, C 25r.

2 St John Damascene, *De fide orth.* 3, 24: PG 94, 1089C.

3 *Ps* 130:1.

4 Cf. *Lk* 18:9-14.

5 *Rom* 8:26.

6 St Augustine, *Sermo* 56, 6, 9: PL 38, 381.

7 *Jn* 4:10.

8 Cf. St Augustine, *De diversis quaestionibus octoginta tribus* 64, 4: PL 40, 56.

living water.'[9] Paradoxically our prayer of petition is a response to the plea of the living God: 'They have forsaken me, the fountain of living waters and hewn out cisterns for themselves, broken cisterns that can hold no water!'[10] Prayer is the response of faith to the free promise of salvation and also a response of love to the thirst of the only Son of God.[11]

Prayer as covenant

2562 Where does prayer come from? Whether prayer is expressed in words or gestures, it is the whole man who prays. But in naming the source of prayer, Scripture speaks sometimes of the soul or the spirit, but most often of the heart (more than a thousand times). According to Scripture, it is the *heart* that prays. If our heart is far from God, the words of prayer are in vain.

2563 The heart is the dwelling-place where I am, where I live; according to the Semitic or Biblical expression, the heart is the place 'to which I withdraw.' The heart is our hidden centre, beyond the grasp of our reason and of others; only the Spirit of God can fathom the human heart and know it fully. The heart is the place of decision, deeper than our psychic drives. It is the place of truth, where we choose life or death. It is the place of encounter, because as 1696, 2699 image of God we live in relation: it is the place of covenant.

2564 Christian prayer is a covenant relationship between God and man in Christ. It is the action of God and of man, springing forth from both the Holy Spirit and ourselves, wholly directed to the Father, in union with the human will of the Son of God made man.

Prayer as communion

2565 In the New Covenant, prayer is the living relationship of the children of God with their Father who is good beyond measure, with his Son Jesus Christ and with the Holy Spirit. The grace of the Kingdom is 'the union of the entire holy and royal Trinity ... with 260 the whole human spirit.'[12] Thus, the life of prayer is the habit of being in the presence of the thrice-holy God and in communion with him. This communion of life is always possible because, through Baptism, we have already been united with Christ.[13] Prayer is *Christian* insofar as it is communion with Christ and extends throughout the Church, which is his Body. Its dimensions are those of Christ's 792 love.[14]

---

9 *Jn* 4:10.
10 *Jer* 2:13.
11 Cf. *Jn* 7:37-39; 19:28; *Is* 12:3; 51:1; *Zech* 12:10; 13:1.

12 St Gregory of Nazianzus, *Oratio*, 16, 9: PG 35, 945.
13 Cf. *Rom* 6:5.
14 Cf. *Eph* 3:18-21.

CHAPTER ONE

THE REVELATION OF PRAYER

THE UNIVERSAL CALL TO PRAYER

2566 *Man is in search of God.* In the act of creation, God calls every being from nothingness into existence. 'Crowned with glory and honour', man is, after the angels, capable of acknowledging 'how majestic is the name of the Lord in all the earth.'[1] Even after losing through his sin his likeness to God, man remains an image of his Creator, and retains the desire for the one who calls him into existence. All religions bear witness to men's essential search for God.[2]

2567 *God calls man first.* Man may forget his Creator or hide far from his face; he may run after idols or accuse the deity of having abandoned him; yet the living and true God tirelessly calls each person to that mysterious encounter known as prayer. In prayer, the faithful God's initiative of love always comes first; our own first step is always a response. As God gradually reveals himself and reveals man to himself, prayer appears as a reciprocal call, a covenant drama. Through words and actions, this drama engages the heart. It unfolds throughout the whole history of salvation.

296

355

28

30

142

ARTICLE 1

In the Old Testament

2568 In the Old Testament, the revelation of prayer comes between the fall and the restoration of man, that is, between God's sorrowful call to his first children: 'Where are you? ... What is this that you have done?'[3] and the response of God's only Son on coming into the world: 'Lo, I have come to do your will, O God.'[4] Prayer is bound up with human history, for it is the relationship with God in historical events.

410
1736

2738

Creation – source of prayer

2569 Prayer is lived in the first place beginning with the realities of *creation*. The first nine chapters of Genesis describe this relationship with God as an offering of the first-born of Abel's flock, as the invocation of the divine name at the time of Enosh, and as 'walking with God.'[5] Noah's offering is pleasing to God, who blesses him and through him all creation, because his heart was upright and undi-

288

58

---

1 *Ps* 8:6; 8:1.
2 Cf. *Acts* 17:27.
3 *Gen* 3:9,13.

4 *Heb* 10:5–7.
5 Cf. *Gen* 4:4, 26; *Gen* 5:24.

vided; Noah, like Enoch before him, 'walks with God.'[6] This kind of prayer is lived by many righteous people in all religions.

In his indefectible covenant with every living creature,[7] God has always called people to prayer. But it is above all beginning with our father Abraham that prayer is revealed in the Old Testament.

59

God's promise and the prayer of faith

145

2570 When God calls him, Abraham goes forth 'as the Lord had told him';[8] Abraham's heart is entirely submissive to the Word and so he obeys. Such attentiveness of the heart, whose decisions are made according to God's will, is essential to prayer, while the words used count only in relation to it. Abraham's prayer is expressed first by deeds: a man of silence, he constructs an altar to the Lord at each stage of his journey. Only later does Abraham's first prayer in words appear: a veiled complaint reminding God of his promises which seem unfulfilled.[9] Thus one aspect of the drama of prayer appears from the beginning: the test of faith in the fidelity of God.

494

2635

2571 Because Abraham believed in God and walked in his presence and in covenant with him,[10] the patriarch is ready to welcome a mysterious Guest into his tent. Abraham's remarkable hospitality at Mamre foreshadows the annunciation of the true Son of the promise.[11] After that, once God had confided his plan, Abraham's heart is attuned to his Lord's compassion for men and he dares to intercede for them with bold confidence.[12]

603

2572 As a final stage in the purification of his faith, Abraham, 'who had received the promises,'[13] is asked to sacrifice the son God had given him. Abraham's faith does not weaken ('God himself will provide the lamb for a burnt offering'), for he 'considered that God was able to raise men even from the dead.'[14] And so the father of believers is conformed to the likeness of the Father who will not spare his own Son but will deliver him up for us all.[15] Prayer restores man to God's likeness and enables him to share in the power of God's love that saves the multitude.[16]

2573 God renews his promise to Jacob, the ancestor of the twelve tribes of Israel.[17] Before confronting his elder brother Esau, Jacob wrestles all night with a mysterious figure who refuses to reveal his name, but he blesses him before leaving him at dawn. From this

---

6 Gen 6:9; 8:20–9:17.
7 Gen 9:8-16.
8 Gen 12:4.
9 Cf. Gen 15:2f.
10 Cf. Gen 15:6; 17:1f.
11 Cf. Gen 18:1–15; Lk 1:26–38.
12 Cf. Gen 18:16–33.
13 Heb 11:17.
14 Gen 22:8; Heb 11:19.
15 Rom 8:32.
16 Cf. Rom 8:16–21.
17 Cf. Gen 28:10–22.

account, the spiritual tradition of the Church has retained the symbol of prayer as a battle of faith and as the triumph of perseverance.[18]

162

Moses and the prayer of the mediator

2574 Once the promise begins to be fulfilled (Passover, the Exodus, the gift of the Law and the ratification of the covenant), the prayer of Moses becomes the most striking example of intercessory prayer, which will be fulfilled in 'the one mediator between God and men, the man Christ Jesus.' [19]

62

2575 Here again the initiative is God's. From the midst of the burning bush he calls Moses.[20] This event will remain one of the primordial images of prayer in the spiritual tradition of Jews and Christians alike. When 'the God of Abraham, of Isaac and of Jacob' calls Moses to be his servant, it is because he is the living God who wants men to live. God reveals himself in order to save them, though he does not do this alone or despite them: he calls Moses to be his messenger, an associate in his compassion, his work of salvation. There is something of a divine plea in this mission, and only after long debate does Moses attune his own will to that of the Saviour God. But in the dialogue in which God confides in him, Moses also learns how to pray: he balks, makes excuses, above all questions: and it is in response to his question that the Lord confides his ineffable name, which will be revealed through his mighty deeds.

205

2576 'Thus the LORD used to speak to Moses face to face, as a man speaks to his friend.' [21] Moses' prayer is characteristic of contemplative prayer by which God's servant remains faithful to his mission. Moses converses with God often and at length, climbing the mountain to hear and entreat him and coming down to the people to repeat the words of his God for their guidance. Moses 'is entrusted with all my house. With him I speak face to face, clearly, not in riddles', for 'Moses was very humble, more so than anyone else on the face of the earth.' [22]

555

2577 From this intimacy with the faithful God, slow to anger and abounding in steadfast love,[23] Moses drew strength and determination for his intercession. He does not pray for himself but for the people whom God made his own. Moses already intercedes for them during the battle with the Amalekites and prays to obtain healing for Miriam.[24] But it is chiefly after their apostasy that Moses 'stands

210

2635

---

18 Cf. Gen 32:24-30; Lk 18:1-8.
19 1 Tim 2:5.
20 Ex 3:1-10.
21 Ex 33:11.

22 Num 12:3, 7-8.
23 Cf. Ex 34:6.
24 Cf. Ex 17:8-12; Num 12:13-14.

214

in the breach' before God in order to save the people.[25] The arguments of his prayer – for intercession is also a mysterious battle – will inspire the boldness of the great intercessors among the Jewish people and in the Church: God is love; he is therefore righteous and faithful; he cannot contradict himself; he must remember his marvellous deeds, since his glory is at stake, and he cannot forsake this people that bears his name.

David and the prayer of the king

2578 The prayer of the People of God flourishes in the shadow of God's dwelling place, first the ark of the covenant and later the Temple. At first the leaders of the people – the shepherds and the prophets – teach them to pray. The infant Samuel must have learned from his mother Hannah how 'to stand before the LORD' and from the priest Eli how to listen to his word: 'Speak, LORD, for your servant is listening.'[26] Later, he will also know the cost and consequence of intercession: 'Moreover, as for me, far be it from me that I should sin against the LORD by ceasing to pray for you; and I will instruct you in the good and the right way.'[27]

709

436

2579 David is *par excellence* the king 'after God's own heart', the shepherd who prays for his people and prays in their name. His submission to the will of God, his praise and his repentance, will be a model for the prayer of the people. His prayer, the prayer of God's Anointed, is a faithful adherence to the divine promise and expresses a loving and joyful trust in God, the only King and Lord.[28] In the Psalms, David, inspired by the Holy Spirit, is the first prophet of Jewish and Christian prayer. The prayer of Christ, the true Messiah and Son of David, will reveal and fulfil the meaning of this prayer.

583

2580 The Temple of Jerusalem, the house of prayer that David wanted to build, will be the work of his son, Solomon. The prayer at the dedication of the Temple relies on God's promise and covenant, on the active presence of his name among his People, recalling his mighty deeds at the Exodus.[29] The king lifts his hands toward heaven and begs the Lord, on his own behalf, on behalf of the entire people and of the generations yet to come, for the forgiveness of their sins and for their daily needs, so that the nations may know that He is the only God and that the heart of his people may belong wholly and entirely to him.

---

25 Ps. 106:23; cf. Ex 32:1-34:9.   28 Cf. 2 Sam 7:18-29.

26 1 Sam 3:9-10; cf. 1:9-18 .   29 1 Kings 8:10-61.

27 1 Sam 12:23.

Elijah, the prophets and conversion of heart

2581 For the People of God, the Temple was to be the place of their education in prayer: pilgrimages, feasts and sacrifices, the evening offering, the incense, and the bread of the Presence ('shewbread') – all these signs of the holiness and glory of God Most High and Most Near were appeals to and ways of prayer. But ritualism often encouraged an excessively external worship. The people needed education in faith and conversion of heart; this was the mission of the prophets, both before and after the Exile.

1150

2582 Elijah is the 'father' of the prophets, 'the generation of those who seek him, who seek the face of the God of Jacob.'[30] Elijah's name, 'The Lord is my God', foretells the people's cry in response to his prayer on Mount Carmel.[31] St James refers to Elijah in order to encourage us to pray: 'The prayer of the righteous is powerful and effective.'[32]

2583 After Elijah had learned mercy during his retreat at the Wadi Cherith, he teaches the widow of Zarephath to believe in The Word of God and confirms her faith by his urgent prayer: God brings the widow's child back to life.[33]

The sacrifice on Mount Carmel is a decisive test for the faith of the People of God. In response to Elijah's plea, 'Answer me, O LORD, answer me', the Lord's fire consumes the holocaust, at the time of the evening oblation. The Eastern liturgies repeat Elijah's plea in the Eucharistic *epiclesis*.

696

Finally, taking the desert road that leads to the place where the living and true God reveals himself to his people, Elijah, like Moses before him, hides 'in a cleft of the rock' until the mysterious presence of God has passed by.[34] But only on the mountain of the Transfiguration will Moses and Elijah behold the unveiled face of him whom they sought; 'the light of the knowledge of the glory of God [shines] in the face of Christ', crucified and risen.[35]

555

2584 In their 'one to one' encounters with God, the prophets draw light and strength for their mission. Their prayer is not flight from this unfaithful world, but rather attentiveness to the Word of God. At times their prayer is an argument or a complaint, but it is always an intercession that awaits and prepares for the intervention of the Saviour God, the Lord of history.[36]

2709

---

30 Ps 24:6.
31 1 *Kings* 18:39.
32 *Jas* 5:16b-18 .
33 Cf. 1 *Kings* 17:7-24.

34 Cf. 1 *Kings* 19:1-14; cf. *Ex* 33:19-23.
35 2 *Cor* 4:6; cf. *Lk* 9:30-35.
36 Cf. *Am* 7:2,5; *Is* 6:5,8,11; *Jer* 1:6;
15:15-18; 20:7-18.

The Psalms, the prayer of the assembly

2585 From the time of David to the coming of the Messiah texts appearing in these sacred books show a deepening in prayer for oneself and in prayer for others.[37] Thus the Psalms were gradually collected into the five books of the Psalter (or 'Praises'), the masterwork of prayer in the Old Testament.

1093

2586 The Psalms both nourished and expressed the prayer of the People of God gathered during the great feasts at Jerusalem and each Sabbath in the synagogues. Their prayer is inseparably personal and communal; it concerns both those who are praying, and all men. The Psalms arose from the communities of the Holy Land and the Diaspora, but embrace all creation. Their prayer recalls the saving events of the past, yet extends into the future, even to the end of history; it commemorates the promises God has already kept, and awaits the Messiah who will fulfil them definitively. Prayed by Christ and fulfilled in him, the Psalms remain essential to the prayer of the Church.[38]

1177

2587 The Psalter is the book in which The Word of God becomes man's prayer. In other books of the Old Testament, 'the words proclaim [God's] works and bring to light the mystery they contain.'[39] The words of the Psalmist, sung for God, both express and acclaim the Lord's saving works; the same Spirit inspires both God's work and man's response. Christ will unite the two. In him, the psalms continue to teach us how to pray.

2641

2588 The Psalter's many forms of prayer take shape both in the liturgy of the Temple and in the human heart. Whether hymns or prayers of lamentation or thanksgiving, whether individual or communal, whether royal chants, songs of pilgrimage or wisdom-meditations, the Psalms are a mirror of God's marvellous deeds in the history of his people, as well as reflections of the human experiences of the Psalmist. Though a given psalm may reflect an event of the past, it still possesses such direct simplicity that it can be prayed in truth by men of all times and conditions.

2589 Certain constant characteristics appear throughout the Psalms: simplicity and spontaneity of prayer; the desire for God himself through and with all that is good in his creation; the distraught situation of the believer who, in his preferential love for the Lord, is exposed to a host of enemies and temptations, but who waits upon what the faithful God will do, in the certitude of his love and in submission to his will. The prayer of the Psalms is always sustained

304

---

37 Ezra 9:6-15; Neh 1:4-11; Jn 2:3-10;   38 Cf. GILH, nn. 100-109.
Tob 3:11-16; Jdt 9:2- 14.   39 DV 2.

by praise; that is why the title of this collection as handed down to us is so fitting: 'The Praises.' Collected for the assembly's worship, the Psalter both sounds the call to prayer and sings the response to that call: *Hallelu-Yah*! ('Alleluia'), 'Praise the Lord!'

> What is more pleasing than a psalm? David expresses it well: 'Praise the Lord, for a psalm is good: let there be praise of our God with gladness and grace!' Yes, a psalm is a blessing on the lips of the people, praise of God, the assembly's homage, a general acclamation, a word that speaks for all, the voice of the Church, a confession of faith in song.[40]

IN BRIEF

2590 'Prayer is the raising of one's mind and heart to God or the requesting of good things from God.' (St John Damascene, De fide orth. 3, 24: PG 94, 1089C).

2591 God tirelessly calls each person to this mysterious encounter with Himself. Prayer unfolds throughout the whole history of salvation as a reciprocal call between God and man.

2592 The prayer of Abraham and Jacob is presented as a battle of faith marked by trust in God's faithfulness and by certitude in the victory promised to perseverance.

2593 The prayer of Moses responds to the living God's initiative for the salvation of his people. It foreshadows the prayer of intercession of the unique mediator, Christ Jesus.

2594 The prayer of the People of God flourished in the shadow of the dwelling place of God's presence on earth, the ark of the covenant and the Temple, under the guidance of their shepherds, especially King David, and of the prophets.

2595 The prophets summoned the people to conversion of heart and, while zealously seeking the face of God, like Elijah, they interceded for the people.

2596 The Psalms constitute the masterwork of prayer in the Old Testament. They present two inseparable qualities: the personal, and the communal. They extend to all dimensions of history, recalling God's promises already fulfilled, and looking for the coming of the Messiah.

2597 Prayed and fulfilled in Christ, the Psalms are an essential and permanent element of the prayer of the Church. They are suitable for men of every condition and time.

---

40 St Ambrose, *In psalmum 1 enarratio*, 1,9: PL 14, 924; *LH*, Saturday, wk 10, OR.

ARTICLE 2
In The Fullness of Time

2598 The drama of prayer is fully revealed to us in the Word who became flesh and dwells among us. To seek to understand his prayer through what his witnesses proclaim to us in the Gospel is to approach the holy Lord Jesus as Moses approached the burning bush: first to contemplate him in prayer, then to hear how he teaches us to pray, in order to know how he hears our prayer.

Jesus prays

470

584

534

2599 The Son of God who became Son of the Virgin learned to pray in his human heart. He learns to pray from his mother, who kept all the great things the Almighty had done and treasured them in her heart.[41] He learns to pray in the words and rhythms of the prayer of his people, in the synagogue at Nazareth and the Temple at Jerusalem. But his prayer springs from an otherwise secret source, as he intimates at the age of twelve: 'I must be in my Father's house.'[42] Here the newness of prayer in the fullness of time begins to be revealed: his *filial prayer*, which the Father awaits from his children, is finally going to be lived out by the only Son in his humanity, with and for men.

535, 554

612
858, 442

2600 The Gospel according to St Luke emphasises the action of the Holy Spirit and the meaning of prayer in Christ's ministry. Jesus prays *before* the decisive moments of his mission: before his Father's witness to him during his baptism and Transfiguration, and before his own fulfilment of the Father's plan of love by his Passion.[43] He also prays before the decisive moments involving the mission of his apostles: at his election and call of the Twelve, before Peter's confession of him as 'the Christ of God,' and again that the faith of the chief of the apostles may not fail when tempted.[44] Jesus' prayer before the events of salvation that the Father has asked him to fulfil is a humble and trusting commitment of his human will to the loving will of the Father.

2765

2601 'He was praying in a certain place and when he had ceased, one of his disciples said to him, "Lord, teach us to pray".'[45] In seeing the Master at prayer the disciple of Christ also wants to pray. By *contemplating* and hearing the Son, the master of prayer, the children learn to pray to the Father.

2602 Jesus often draws apart to pray *in solitude*, on a mountain,

---

41 Cf. *Lk* 1:49; 2:19; 2:51.
42 *Lk* 2:49.
43 Cf. *Lk* 3:21; 9:28; 22:32.

44 Cf. *Lk* 6:12; 9:18–20; 22:41-44.
45 *Lk* 11:1.

preferably at night.[46] *He includes all men* in his prayer, for he has taken on humanity in his incarnation, and he offers them to the Father when he offers himself. Jesus, the Word who has become flesh, shares by his human prayer in all that 'his brethren' experience; he sympathises with their weaknesses in order to free them.[47] It was for this that the Father sent him. His words and works are the visible manifestation of his prayer in secret.

2603 The evangelists have preserved two more explicit prayers offered by Christ during his public ministry. Each begins with thanksgiving. In the first, Jesus confesses the Father, acknowledges and blesses him because he has hidden the mysteries of the Kingdom from those who think themselves learned and has revealed them to infants, the poor of the Beatitudes.[48] His exclamation, 'Yes, Father!' expresses the depth of his heart, his adherence to the Father's 'good pleasure', echoing his mother's *Fiat* at the time of his conception and prefiguring what he will say to the Father in his agony. The whole prayer of Jesus is contained in this loving adherence of his human heart to the mystery of the will of the Father.[49]

2604 The second prayer, before the raising of Lazarus, is recorded by St. John.[50] Thanksgiving precedes the event: 'Father, I thank you for having heard me', which implies that the Father always hears his petitions. Jesus immediately adds: 'I know that you always hear me', which implies that Jesus, on his part, *constantly made such petitions*. Jesus' prayer, characterised by thanksgiving, reveals to us how to ask: *before* the gift is given, Jesus commits himself to the One who in giving gives himself. The Giver is more precious than the gift; he is the 'treasure'; in him abides his Son's heart; the gift is given 'as well.'[51]

> The priestly prayer of Jesus holds a unique place in the economy of salvation.[52] A meditation on it will conclude Section One. It reveals the ever present prayer of our High Priest and, at the same time, contains what he teaches us about our prayer to our Father, which will be developed in Section Two.

2605 When the hour had come for him to fulfil the Father's plan of love, Jesus allows a glimpse of the boundless depth of his filial prayer, not only before he freely delivered himself up ('*Abba. ... not my will, but yours*'),[53] but even in *his last words* on the Cross, where prayer and the gift of self are but one: 'Father, forgive them, for they know not what they do';[54] 'Truly, I say to you, today you will be

616

2637

2546

494

478

2746

614

---

46 Cf. *Mk* 1:35; 6:46; *Lk* 5:16.
47 Cf. *Heb* 2:12, 15; 4:15.
48 Cf. *Mt* 11:25–27 and *Lk* 10:21–23.
49 Cf. *Eph* 1:9.
50 Cf. *Jn* 11:41-42.
51 *Mt* 6:21, 33.
52 Cf. *Jn* 17.
53 *Lk* 22:42.
54 *Lk* 23:34.

with me in Paradise';[55] 'Woman, behold your son' – 'Behold your mother';[56] 'I thirst.';[57] 'My God, My God, why have you forsaken me?';[58] 'It is finished';[59] 'Father, into your hands I commit my spirit!'[60] until the 'loud cry' as he expires, giving up his spirit.[61]

403

653

2587

2606 All the troubles, for all time, of humanity enslaved by sin and death, all the petitions and intercessions of salvation history are summed up in this cry of the incarnate Word. Here the Father accepts them and, beyond all hope, answers them by raising his Son. Thus is fulfilled and brought to completion the drama of prayer in the economy of creation and salvation. The Psalter gives us the key to prayer in Christ. In the 'today' of the Resurrection the Father says: 'You are my Son, today I have begotten you. Ask of me, and I will make the nations your heritage, and the ends of the earth your possession.'[62]

> *The Letter to the Hebrews* expresses in dramatic terms how the prayer of Jesus accomplished the victory of salvation: 'In the days of his flesh, Jesus offered up prayers and supplications, with loud cries and tears, to him who was able to save him from death, and he was heard for his godly fear. Although he was a Son, he learned obedience through what he suffered, and being made perfect, he became the source of eternal salvation to all who obey him.'[63]

Jesus teaches us how to pray

520

2607 When Jesus prays he is already teaching us how to pray. His prayer to his Father is the theologal path [the path of faith, hope and charity] of our prayer to God. But the Gospel also gives us Jesus' explicit teaching on prayer. Like a wise teacher he takes hold of us where we are and leads us progressively toward the Father. Addressing the crowds following him, Jesus builds on what they already know of prayer from the Old Covenant and opens to them the newness of the coming Kingdom. Then he reveals this newness to them in parables. Finally, he will speak openly of the Father and the Holy Spirit to his disciples who will be the teachers of prayer in his Church.

541

1430

2608 From the *Sermon on the Mount* onwards, Jesus insists on *conversion of heart*: reconciliation with one's brother before presenting an offering on the altar, love of enemies and prayer for persecutors, prayer to the Father in secret, not heaping up empty phrases, prayerful forgiveness from the depths of the heart, purity of heart and seeking

---

55 *Lk* 23:43.
56 *Jn* 19:26-27.
57 *Jn* 19:28.
58 *Mk* 15:34; cf. *Ps* 22:2.
59 *Jn* 19:30.

60 *Lk* 23:46.
61 Cf. *Mk* 15:37; *Jn* 19:30b.
62 *Ps* 2:7–8; cf. *Acts* 13:33.
63 *Heb* 5:7–9.

the Kingdom before all else.[64] This filial conversion is entirely directed to the Father.

2609 Once committed to conversion, the heart learns to pray in *faith*. Faith is a filial adherence to God beyond what we feel and understand. It is possible because the beloved Son gives us access to the Father. He can ask us to 'seek' and to 'knock', since he himself is the door and the way.[65]

153, 1814

2610 Just as Jesus prays to the Father and gives thanks before receiving his gifts, so he teaches us *filial boldness*: 'Whatever you ask in prayer, believe that you receive it, and you will.'[66] Such is the power of prayer and of faith that does not doubt: 'all things are possible to him who believes.'[67] Jesus is as saddened by the 'lack of faith' of his own neighbours and the 'little faith' of his own disciples[68] as he is struck with admiration at the great faith of the Roman centurion and the Canaanite woman.[69]

165

2611 The prayer of faith consists not only in saying 'Lord, Lord', but in disposing the heart to do the will of the Father.[70] Jesus calls his disciples to bring into their prayer this concern for co–operating with the divine plan.[71]

2827

2612 In Jesus 'the Kingdom of God is at hand.'[72] He calls his hearers to conversion and faith, but also to *watchfulness*. In prayer the disciple keeps watch, attentive to Him Who Is and Him Who Comes, in memory of his first coming in the lowliness of the flesh, and in the hope of his second coming in glory.[73] In communion with their Master, the disciples' prayer is a battle; only by keeping watch in prayer can one avoid falling into temptation.[74]

672

2725

2613 Three principal *parables* on prayer are transmitted to us by St Luke:
– The first, 'the importunate friend',[75] invites us to urgent prayer: 'Knock, and it will be opened to you.' To the one who prays like this, the heavenly Father will 'give whatever he needs', and above all the Holy Spirit who contains all gifts.

546

– The second, 'the importunate widow',[76] is centred on one of the qualities of prayer: it is necessary to pray always without ceasing, and with the *patience* of faith. 'And yet, when the Son of Man comes, will he find faith on earth?'

---

64 Cf. *Mt* 5:23-24, 44-45; 6:7, 14–15, 21, 25, 33.
65 Cf. *Mt* 7:7–11, 13-14.
66 *Mk* 11:24.
67 *Mk* 9:23; cf. *Mt* 21:22.
68 Cf. *Mk* 6:6; *Mt* 8:26.
69 Cf. *Mt* 8:10; 15:28.
70 Cf. *Mt* 7:21.
71 Cf. *Mt* 9:38; *Lk* 10:2; *Jn* 4:34.
72 *Mk* 1:15.
73 Cf. *Mk* 13; *Lk* 21:34-36.
74 Cf. *Lk* 22:40, 46.
75 Cf. *Lk* 11:5–13.
76 Cf. *Lk* 18:1-8.

2559   – The third parable, 'the Pharisee and the tax collector',[77] concerns the *humility* of the heart that prays. 'God, be merciful to me a sinner!' The Church continues to make this prayer its own: *Kyrie eleison!*

434

2614 When Jesus openly entrusts to his disciples the mystery of prayer to the Father he reveals to them what their prayer and ours must be, once he has returned to the Father in his glorified humanity. What is new is to 'ask *in his name.*'[78] Faith in the Son introduces the disciples into the knowledge of the Father, because Jesus is 'the way, and the truth, and the life.'[79] Faith bears its fruit in love: it means keeping the word and the commandments of Jesus, it means abiding with him in the Father who, in him, so loves us that he abides with us. In this new covenant the certitude that our petitions will be heard is founded on the prayer of Jesus.[80]

728

2615 Even more, what the Father gives us when our prayer is united with that of Jesus is 'another Counsellor, to be with you for ever, the Spirit of truth.'[81] This new dimension of prayer and of its circumstances is displayed throughout the farewell discourse.[82] In the Holy Spirit, Christian prayer is a communion of love with the Father, not only through Christ but also *in him*: 'Hitherto you have asked nothing in my name; ask, and you will receive, that your joy may be full.'[83]

Jesus hears our prayer

548

2616 Prayer *to Jesus* is answered by him already during his ministry, through signs that anticipate the power of his death and Resurrection: Jesus hears the prayer of faith, expressed in words (the leper, Jairus, the Canaanite woman, the good thief)[84] or in silence (the bearers of the paralytic, the woman with a haemorrhage who touches his clothes, the tears and ointment of the sinful woman).[85] The urgent request of the blind men, 'Have mercy on us, Son of David' or 'Jesus, Son of David, have mercy on me!'[86] has been

2667

renewed in the traditional prayer to Jesus known as the *Jesus Prayer*: 'Lord Jesus Christ, Son of God, have mercy on me, a sinner!' Healing infirmities or forgiving sins, Jesus always responds to a prayer offered in faith: 'Your faith has made you well; go in peace.'

St. Augustine wonderfully summarises the three dimensions of Jesus' prayer: 'He prays for us as our priest, prays in us as our Head, and is

---

77 Cf. *Lk* 18:9-14.
78 *Jn* 14:13.
79 *Jn* 14:6.
80 Cf. *Jn* 14:13-14.
81 *Jn* 14:16-17.
82 Cf. *Jn* 14:23-26; 15:7. 16; 16:

13-15; 16:23-27.
83 *Jn* 16:24.
84 Cf. *Mk* 1:40-41; 5:36; 7:29;
    Cf. *Lk* 23:39-43.
85 Cf. *Mk* 2:5; 5:28; *Lk* 7:37-38.
86 *Mt* 9:27; *Mk* 10:48.

prayed to by us as our God. Therefore let us acknowledge our voice in him and his in us.'[87]

The prayer of the Virgin Mary

2617 Mary's prayer is revealed to us at the dawning of the fullness of time. Before the incarnation of the Son of God, and before the outpouring of the Holy Spirit, her prayer cooperates in a unique way with the Father's plan of loving kindness: at the Annunciation, for Christ's conception; at Pentecost, for the formation of the Church, his Body.[88] In the faith of his humble handmaid, the Gift of God found the acceptance he had awaited from the beginning of time. She whom the Almighty made 'full of grace' responds by offering her whole being: 'Behold I am the handmaid of the Lord; let it be [done] to me according to your word.' 'Fiat': this is Christian prayer: to be wholly God's, because he is wholly ours.

148

494

490

2618 The Gospel reveals to us how Mary prays and intercedes in faith. At Cana,[89] the mother of Jesus asks her son for the needs of a wedding feast; this is the sign of another feast – that of the wedding of the Lamb where he gives his body and blood at the request of the Church, his Bride. It is at the hour of the New Covenant, at the foot of the cross,[90] that Mary is heard as the Woman, the new Eve, the true 'Mother of all the living.'

2674

726

2619 That is why the Canticle of Mary,[91] the *Magnificat* (Latin) or *Megalynei* (Byzantine) is the song both of the Mother of God and of the Church; the song of the Daughter of Zion and of the new People of God; the song of thanksgiving for the fullness of graces poured out in the economy of salvation and the song of the 'poor' whose hope is met by the fulfilment of the promises made to our ancestors, 'to Abraham and to his posterity for ever'.

724

IN BRIEF

2620 Jesus' filial prayer is the perfect model of prayer in the New Testament. Often done in solitude and in secret, the prayer of Jesus involves a loving adherence to the will of the Father even to the Cross and an absolute confidence in being heard.

2621 In his teaching, Jesus teaches his disciples to pray with a purified heart, with lively and persevering faith, with filial bold-ness. He calls them to vigilance and invites them to present their petitions to God in his name. Jesus Christ himself answers prayers addressed to him.

---

87 St Augustine, *En. in Ps.* 85, 1:
   PL 37, 1081; cf. GILH 7.
88 Cf. *Lk* 1:38; *Acts* 1:14.

89 Cf. *Jn* 2:1-12.
90 Cf. *Jn* 19:25-27.
91 Cf. *Lk* 1:46-55.

> 2622 The prayers of the Virgin Mary, in her Fiat and Magnificat, are characterised by the generous offering of her whole being in faith.

ARTICLE 3
In the Age of the Church

731

2623 On the day of Pentecost, the Spirit of the Promise was poured out on the disciples, gathered 'together in one place.'[92] While awaiting the Spirit, 'all these with one accord devoted themselves to prayer.'[93] The Spirit who teaches the Church and recalls for her everything that Jesus said[94] was also to form her in the life of prayer.

1342

2624 In the first community of Jerusalem, believers 'devoted themselves to the apostles' teaching and fellowship, to the breaking of bread and the prayers.'[95] This sequence is characteristic of the Church's prayer: founded on the apostolic faith; authenticated by charity; nourished in the Eucharist.

2625 In the first place these are prayers that the faithful hear and read in the Scriptures, but also that they make their own – especially those of the Psalms, in view of their fulfilment in Christ.[96] The Holy Spirit, who thus keeps the memory of Christ alive in his Church at prayer, also leads her toward the fullness of truth and inspires new formulations expressing the unfathomable mystery of Christ at work in his Church's life, sacraments and mission. These formulations are developed in the great liturgical and spiritual traditions. The *forms of prayer* revealed in the apostolic and canonical Scriptures remain normative for Christian prayer.

1092

1200

I. Blessing and Adoration

1078

2626 *Blessing* expresses the basic movement of Christian prayer: it is an encounter between God and man. In blessing, God's gift and man's acceptance of it are united in dialogue with each other. The prayer of blessing is man's response to God's gifts: because God blesses, the human heart can in return bless the One who is the source of every blessing.

1083

2627 Two fundamental forms express this movement: our prayer *ascends* in the Holy Spirit through Christ to the Father – we bless him for having blessed us;[97] it implores the grace of the Holy Spirit that *descends* through Christ from the Father – he blesses us.[98]

---

92 *Acts* 2:1.
93 *Acts* 1:14.
94 Cf. *Jn* 14:26.
95 *Acts* 2:42.

96 Cf. *Lk* 24:27, 44.
97 Cf. *Eph* 1:3-14; 2 *Cor* 1:3-7; 1 *Pt* 1:3-9.
98 Cf. 2 *Cor* 13:13; *Rom* 15:5-6, 13; *Eph* 6:23-24.

2628 *Adoration* is the first attitude of man acknowledging that he is 2096–2097
a creature before his Creator. It exalts the greatness of the Lord who
made us[99] and the almighty power of the Saviour who sets us free
from evil. Adoration is homage of the spirit to the 'King of Glory',[100]
respectful silence in the presence of the 'ever greater' God.[101] Adoration of the thrice-holy and sovereign God of love blends with humil-   2559
ity and gives assurance to our supplications.

II. Prayer of Petition

2629 The vocabulary of supplication in the New Testament is rich
in shades of meaning: ask, beseech, plead, invoke, entreat, cry out,
even 'struggle in prayer.'[102] Its most usual form, because the most
spontaneous, is petition: by prayer of petition we express awareness
of our relationship with God. We are creatures who are not our own
beginning, not the masters of adversity, not our own last end. We   396
are sinners who as Christians know that we have turned away from
our Father. Our petition is already a turning back to him.

2630 The New Testament contains scarcely any prayers of lamentation,
so frequent in the Old Testament. In the risen Christ the Church's petition   2090
is buoyed by hope, even if we still wait in a state of expectation and must
be converted anew every day. Christian petition, what St. Paul calls 'groan-
ing', arises from another depth, that of creation 'in labour pains' and that
of ourselves 'as we wait for the redemption of our bodies. For in this hope
we were saved.'[103] In the end, however, the Holy Spirit 'helps us in our
weakness; for we do not know how to pray as we ought, but the Spirit
himself intercedes for us with sighs too deep for words.'[104]

2631 The first movement of the prayer of petition is *asking forgive-*   2838
ness, like the tax collector in the parable: 'God, be merciful to me a
sinner!'[105] It is a prerequisite for righteous and pure prayer. A trusting humility brings us back into the light of communion between the
Father and his Son Jesus Christ and with one another, so that 'we
receive from him whatever we ask.'[106] Asking forgiveness is the
prerequisite for both the Eucharistic liturgy and personal prayer.

2632 Christian petition is centred on the desire and *search for the*
Kingdom to come, in keeping with the teaching of Christ.[107] There is   2816
a hierarchy in these petitions: we pray first for the Kingdom, then
for what is necessary to welcome it and co–operate with its coming.   1942

99 Cf. *Ps.* 95:1-6.
100 *Ps* 24, 9-10.
101 Cf. St Augustine, *En. in Ps.* 62, 16:
      PL 36, 757-758.
102 Cf. *Rom* 15:30; *Col* 4:12.
103 *Rom* 8:22-24.
104 *Rom* 8:26.
105 *Lk* 18:13.
106 *1 Jn* 3:22; cf. 1:7-2:2..
107 Cf. *Mt* 6:10, 33; *Lk* 11:2, 13.

2854

This collaboration with the mission of Christ and the Holy Spirit, which is now that of the Church, is the object of the prayer of the apostolic community.[108] It is the prayer of Paul, the apostle *par excellence*, which reveals to us how the divine solicitude for all the churches ought to inspire Christian prayer.[109] By prayer every baptised person works for the coming of the Kingdom.

2830

2633 When we share in God's saving love, we understand that *every need* can become the object of petition. Christ, who assumed all things in order to redeem all things, is glorified by what we ask the Father in his name.[110] It is with this confidence that St James and St Paul exhort us to pray *at all times*.[111]

III. Prayer of Intercession

432

2634 Intercession is a prayer of petition which leads us to pray as Jesus did. He is the one intercessor with the Father on behalf of all men, especially sinners.[112] He is 'able for all time to save those who draw near to God through him, since he always lives to make intercession for them.'[113] The Holy Spirit 'himself intercedes for us ... and intercedes for the saints according to the will of God.'[114]

2571

2577

2635 Since Abraham, intercession – asking on behalf of another – has been characteristic of a heart attuned to God's mercy. In the age of the Church, Christian intercession participates in Christ's, as an expression of the communion of saints. In intercession, he who prays looks 'not only to his own interests, but also to the interests of others', even to the point of praying for those who do him harm.[115]

1900
1037

2636 The first Christian communities lived this form of fellowship intensely.[116] Thus the Apostle Paul gives them a share in his ministry of preaching the Gospel[117] but also intercedes for them.[118] The intercession of Christians recognizes no boundaries: 'for all men, for kings and all who are in high positions', for persecutors, for the salvation of those who reject the Gospel.[119]

IV. Prayer of Thanksgiving

224
1328

2637 Thanksgiving characterizes the prayer of the Church which, in celebrating the Eucharist, reveals and becomes more fully what

---

108 Cf. *Acts* 6:6; 13:3.
109 Cf. *Rom* 10:1; *Eph* 1:16-23; *Phil* 1:9-11; *Col* 1:3-6; 4:3-4, 12.
110 Cf. *Jn* 14:13.
111 Cf. *Jas* 1:5-8; *Eph* 5:20; *Phil* 4:6-7; *Col* 3:16-17; 1 *Thess* 5:17-18.
112 Cf. *Rom* 8:34; 1 *Jn* 2:1; 1 *Tim* 2:5-8.
113 *Heb* 7:25.

114 *Rom* 8:26-27.
115 *Phil* 2:4; cf. *Acts* 7:60; *Lk* 23:28, 34.
116 Cf. *Acts* 12:5; 20:36; 21:5; 2 *Cor* 9:14.
117 Cf. *Eph* 6:18-20; *Col* 4:3-4; 1 *Thess* 5:25.
118 Cf. 2 *Thess* 1:11; *Col* 1:3; *Phil* 1:3-4.
119 1 *Tim* 2:1; cf. *Rom* 12:14; 10:1.

she is. Indeed, in the work of salvation, Christ sets creation free
from sin and death to consecrate it anew and make it return to the   2603
Father, for his glory. The thanksgiving of the members of the Body
participates in that of their Head.

2638 As in the prayer of petition, every event and need can become
an offering of thanksgiving. The letters of St Paul often begin and
end with thanksgiving, and the Lord Jesus is always present in it:
'Give thanks in all circumstances; for this is the will of God in Christ
Jesus for you'; 'Continue steadfastly in prayer, being watchful in it
with thanksgiving.' [120]

V. Prayer of Praise

2639 Praise is the form of prayer which recognises most immediately that God is God. It lauds God for his own sake and gives him
glory, quite beyond what he does, but simply because HE IS. It shares   213
in the blessed happiness of the pure of heart who love God in faith
before seeing him in glory. By praise, the Spirit is joined to our
spirits to bear witness that we are children of God,[121] testifying to
the only Son in whom we are adopted and by whom we glorify the
Father. Praise embraces the other forms of prayer and carries them
toward him who is its source and goal: the 'one God, the Father,
from whom are all things and for whom we exist.' [122]

2640 St Luke in his gospel often expresses wonder and praise at the mar-
vels of Christ and in his *Acts of the Apostles* stresses them as actions of the
Holy Spirit: the community of Jerusalem, the invalid healed by Peter and
John, the crowd that gives glory to God for that, and the pagans of Pisidia
who 'were glad and glorified the word of God.' [123]

2641 '[Address] one another in psalms and hymns and spiritual songs,
singing and making melody to the Lord with all your heart.' [124] Like the
inspired writers of the New Testament, the first Christian communities
read the Book of Psalms in a new way, singing in it the mystery of Christ.   2587
In the newness of the Spirit, they also composed hymns and canticles in the
light of the unheard-of event that God accomplished in his Son: his Incarnation, his death which conquered death, his Resurrection and Ascension
to the right hand of the Father.[125] Doxology, the praise of God, arises from
this 'marvellous work' of the whole economy of salvation.[126]

---

120 1 *Thess* 5:18; *Col* 4:2.
121 Cf. *Rom* 8:16.
122 1 *Cor* 8:6.
123 *Acts* 2:47; 3:9; 4:21;13:48.
124 *Eph* 5:19; *Col* 3:16.

125 Cf. *Phil* 2:6-11; *Col* 1:15-20;
     Eph 5:14; *1 Tim* 3:16; 6:15-16;
     2 Tim 2:11-13.
126 Cf. *Eph* 1:3-14; *Rom* 16:25-27;
     Eph 3:20-21; *Jude* 24-25.

1137

2642 The *Revelation* of 'what must soon take place', the *Apocalypse*, is borne along by the songs of the heavenly liturgy[127] but also by the intercession of the 'witnesses' (martyrs).[128] The prophets and the saints, all those who were slain on earth for their witness to Jesus, the vast throng of those who, having come through the great tribulation, have gone before us into the Kingdom, all sing the praise and glory of him who sits on the throne, and of the Lamb.[129] In communion with them, the Church on earth also sings these songs with faith in the midst of trial. By means of petition and intercession, faith hopes against all hope and gives thanks to the 'Father of lights', from whom 'every perfect gift' comes down.[130] Thus faith is pure praise.

2643 The Eucharist contains and expresses all forms of prayer: it is 'the pure offering' of the whole Body of Christ to the glory of God's name[131] and, according to the traditions of East and West, it is *the* 'sacrifice of praise'.

1330

IN BRIEF

2644 *The Holy Spirit who teaches the Church and recalls to her all that Jesus said also instructs her in the life of prayer, inspiring new expressions of the same basic forms of prayer: blessing, petition, intercession, thanksgiving and praise.*

2645 *Because God blesses the human heart, it can in return bless him who is the source of every blessing.*

2646 *Forgiveness, the quest for the Kingdom, and every true need are objects of the prayer of petition.*

2647 *Prayer of intercession consists in asking on behalf of another. It knows no boundaries and extends to one's enemies.*

2648 *Every joy and suffering, every event and need can become the matter for thanksgiving which, sharing in that of Christ, should fill one's whole life: 'Give thanks in all circumstances.' (1 Th 5:18)*

2649 *Prayer of praise is entirely disinterested and rises to God, lauds him and gives him glory for his own sake, quite beyond what he has done, but simply because HE IS.*

---

127 Cf. *Rev* 4:8-11; 5:9-14; 7:10-12.   130 *Jas* 1:17.
128 *Rev* 6:10.   131 Cf. *Mal* 1:11.
129 Cf. *Rev* 18:24; 19:1-8.

CHAPTER TWO
THE TRADITION OF PRAYER

2650 Prayer cannot be reduced to the spontaneous outpouring of interior impulse: in order to pray, one must have the will to pray. Nor is it enough to know what the Scriptures reveal about prayer: one must also learn how to pray. Through a living transmission (Sacred Tradition) within 'the believing and praying Church' [1], the Holy Spirit teaches the children of God how to pray.

75

2651 The tradition of Christian prayer is one of the ways in which the tradition of faith takes shape and grows, especially through the contemplation and study of believers who treasure in their hearts the events and words of the economy of salvation, and through their profound grasp of the spiritual realities they experience.[2]

94

ARTICLE 1
At the Wellsprings of Prayer

2652 The Holy Spirit is the *living water* 'welling up to eternal life' [3] in the heart that prays. It is he who teaches us to accept it at its source: Christ. Indeed in the Christian life there are several wellsprings where Christ awaits us to enable us to drink of the Holy Spirit.

694

The Word of God

2653 The Church 'forcefully and specially exhorts all the Christian faithful ... to learn "the surpassing knowledge of Jesus Christ" (*Phil* 3:8) by frequent reading of the divine Scriptures ... Let them remember, however, that prayer should accompany the reading of sacred Scripture, so that a dialogue takes place between God and man. For "we speak to him when we pray; we listen to him when we read the divine oracles." ' [4]

133

1100

2654 The spiritual writers, paraphrasing *Matthew* 7:7, summarize in this way the dispositions of the heart nourished by the Word of God in prayer: 'Seek in reading and you will find in meditating; knock in mental prayer and it will be opened to you by contemplation.' [5]

1 DV 8.
2 Cf. DV 8.
3 Jn 4:14
4 DV 25; cf. Phil 3:8; St Ambrose,

De officiis ministrorum 1, 20, 88:
PL 16, 50.
5 Guigo the Carthusian, *Scala Paradisi*:
PL 40, 998.

The liturgy of the Church

1073 **2655** In the sacramental liturgy of the Church, the mission of Christ and of the Holy Spirit proclaims, makes present and communicates the mystery of salvation, which is continued in the heart that prays. The spiritual writers sometimes compare the heart to an altar. Prayer internalizes and assimilates the liturgy during and after its celebration. Even when it is lived out 'in secret'[6], prayer is always prayer *of the Church*; it is a communion with the Holy Trinity.[7]

1812–1829 ### The theological virtues

368 **2656** One enters into prayer as one enters into liturgy: by the narrow gate of *faith*. Through the signs of his presence, it is the Face of the Lord that we seek and desire; it is his Word that we want to hear and keep.

2657 The Holy Spirit, who instructs us to celebrate the liturgy in expectation of Christ's return, teaches us to pray in *hope*. Conversely, the prayer of the Church and personal prayer nourish hope in us. The Psalms especially, with their concrete and varied language, teach us to fix our hope in God: 'I waited patiently for the LORD; he inclined to me and heard my cry.'[8] As St Paul prayed: 'May the God of hope fill you with all joy and peace in believing, so that by the power of the Holy Spirit you may abound in hope.'[9]

2658 'Hope does not disappoint us, because God's *love* has been poured into our hearts by the Holy Spirit who has been given to us.'[10] Prayer, formed by the liturgical life, draws everything into the love by which we are loved in Christ and which enables us to re826 spond to him by loving as he has loved us. Love is the source of prayer; whoever draws from it reaches the summit of prayer. In the words of the Curé of Ars:

> I love you, O my God, and my only desire is to love you until the last breath of my life. I love you, O my infinitely loveable God, and I would rather die loving you, than live without loving you. I love you, Lord, and the only grace I ask is to love you eternally … My God, if my tongue cannot say in every moment that I love you, I want my heart to repeat it to you as often as I draw breath.[11]

'Today'

1165 **2659** We learn to pray at certain moments by hearing the Word of the Lord and sharing in his Paschal mystery, but his Spirit is offered

---

6 Cf. *Mt* 6:6.
7 *GILH* 9.
8 *Ps* 40:2.
9 *Rom* 15:13.
10 *Rom* 5:5.
11 St John Vianney, *Prayer*.

us at all times, in the events of *each day*, to make prayer spring up from us. Jesus' teaching about praying to our Father is in the same vein as his teaching about providence:[12] time is in the Father's hands; it is in the present that we encounter him, not yesterday nor tomorrow, but today: 'O that *today* you would hearken to his voice! Harden not your hearts.'[13]

2837

305

2660 Prayer in the events of each day and each moment is one of the secrets of the Kingdom revealed to 'little children', to the servants of Christ, to the poor of the Beatitudes. It is right and good to pray so that the coming of the Kingdom of justice and peace may influence the march of history, but it is just as important to bring the help of prayer into humble, everyday situations; all forms of prayer can be the leaven to which the Lord compares the Kingdom.[14]

2546
2632

IN BRIEF

2661 By a living transmission – Tradition – the Holy Spirit in the Church teaches the children of God to pray.

2662 The Word of God, the liturgy of the Church, and the virtues of faith, hope and charity are sources of prayer.

ARTICLE 2
The Way of Prayer

2663 In the living tradition of prayer, each Church proposes to her faithful, according to her historic, social and cultural context, a language for prayer: words, melodies, gestures, iconography. The Magisterium of the Church[15] has the task of discerning the fidelity of these ways of praying to the tradition of apostolic faith; it is for pastors and catechists to explain their meaning, always in relation to Jesus Christ.

1201

Prayer to the Father

2664 There is no other way of Christian prayer than Christ. Whether our prayer is communal or personal, vocal or interior, it has access to the Father only if we pray 'in the name' of Jesus. The sacred humanity of Jesus is therefore the way by which the Holy Spirit teaches us to pray to God our Father.

2780

Prayer to Jesus

2665 The prayer of the Church, nourished by the Word of God and the celebration of the liturgy, teaches us to pray to the Lord Jesus.

451 .

---

12 Cf. *Mt* 6:11, 34.
13 *Ps* 95:7–8.

14 Cf. *Lk* 13:20-21.
15 Cf. *DV* 10.

Even though her prayer is addressed above all to the Father, it includes in all the liturgical traditions forms of prayer addressed to Christ. Certain psalms, given their use in the Prayer of the Church, and the New Testament place on our lips and engrave in our hearts prayer to Christ in the form of invocations: Son of God, Word of God, Lord, Saviour, Lamb of God, King, Beloved Son, Son of the Virgin, Good Shepherd, our Life, our Light, our Hope, our Resurrection, Friend of mankind ...

451

435

2666 But the one name that contains everything is the one that the Son of God received in his incarnation: JESUS. The divine name may not be spoken by human lips, but by assuming our humanity the Word of God hands it over to us and we can invoke it: 'Jesus', 'YAHWEH saves'.[16] The name 'Jesus' contains all: God and man and the whole economy of creation and salvation. To pray 'Jesus' is to invoke him and to call him within us. His name is the only one that contains the presence it signifies. Jesus is the Risen One, and whoever invokes the name of Jesus is welcoming the Son of God who loved him and who gave himself up for him.[17]

2616

2667 This simple invocation of faith developed in the tradition of prayer under many forms in East and West. The most usual formulation, transmitted by the spiritual writers of the Sinai, Syria and Mt Athos, is the invocation, 'Lord Jesus Christ, Son of God, have mercy on us sinners.' It combines the Christological hymn of *Philippians 2:6–11* with the cry of the publican and the blind men begging for light.[18] By it the heart is opened to human wretchedness and the Saviour's mercy.

435

2668 The invocation of the holy name of Jesus is the simplest way of praying always. When the holy name is repeated often by a humbly attentive heart, the prayer is not lost by heaping up empty phrases[19], but holds fast to the Word and 'brings forth fruit with patience.'[20] This prayer is possible 'at all times' because it is not one occupation among others but the only occupation: that of loving God, which animates and transfigures every action in Christ Jesus.

478

1674

2669 The prayer of the Church venerates and honours the *Heart of Jesus* just as it invokes his most holy name. It adores the incarnate Word and his Heart which, out of love for men, he allowed to be pierced by our sins. Christian prayer loves to follow *the way of the cross* in the Saviour's steps. The stations from the Praetorium to Golgotha and the tomb trace the way of Jesus, who by his holy Cross has redeemed the world.

---

16 Cf. *Ex* 3:14; 33:19-23; *Mt.* 1:21.

17 *Rom* 10:13; *Acts* 2:21; 3:15–16; *Gal* 2:20.

18 Cf. *Mk* 10:46–52; *Lk* 18:13.

19 Cf. *Mt* 6:7.

20 Cf. *Lk* 8:15.

'Come, Holy Spirit'

2670 'No one can say "Jesus is Lord" except by the Holy Spirit.'[21]   683
Every time we begin to pray to Jesus it is the Holy Spirit who draws
us on the way of prayer by his prevenient grace. Since he teaches us   2001
to pray by recalling Christ, how could we not pray to the Spirit too?
That is why the Church invites us to call upon the Holy Spirit every   1310
day, especially at the beginning and the end of every important
action.

> If the Spirit should not be worshipped, how can he divinize me through
> Baptism? If he should be worshipped, should he not be the object of
> adoration?[22]

2671 The traditional form of petition to the Holy Spirit is to invoke
the Father through Christ our Lord to give us the Consoler Spirit.[23]
Jesus insists on this petition to be made in his name at the very
moment when he promises the gift of the Spirit of Truth.[24] But the
simplest and most direct prayer is also traditional, 'Come, Holy
Spirit', and every liturgical tradition has developed it in antiphons
and hymns.

> Come, Holy Spirit, fill the hearts of your faithful and enkindle in them
> the fire of your love.[25]

> Heavenly King, Consoler Spirit, Spirit of Truth, present everywhere and
> filling all things, treasure of all good and source of all life, come dwell
> in us, cleanse and save us, you who are All–Good.[26]

2672 The Holy Spirit, whose anointing permeates our whole being,   695
is the interior Master of Christian prayer. He is the artisan of the
living tradition of prayer. To be sure, there are as many paths of
prayer as there are persons who pray, but it is the same Spirit acting
in all and with all. It is in the communion of the Holy Spirit that
Christian prayer is prayer in the Church.

In communion with the holy Mother of God

2673 In prayer the Holy Spirit unites us to the person of the only   689
Son, in his glorified humanity, through which and in which our filial
prayer unites us in the Church with the Mother of Jesus.[27]

2674 Mary gave her consent in faith at the Annunciation and main-   494
tained it without hesitation at the foot of the Cross. Ever since, her

---

21 1 *Cor* 12:3.
22 St Gregory of Nazianzus, *Oratio*,
    31, 28: PG 36, 165.
23 Cf. *Lk* 11:13.
24 Cf. *Jn* 14:17; 15:26; 16:13.

25 *Roman Missal*, Pentecost, Sequence.
26 *Byzantine Liturgy, Pentecost Vespers*,
    Troparion.
27 Cf. *Acts* 1:14.

motherhood has extended to the brothers and sisters of her Son 'who still journey on earth surrounded by dangers and difficulties.'[28] Jesus, the only mediator, is the way of our prayer; Mary, his mother and ours, is wholly transparent to him: she 'shows the way' (*hodigitria*), and is herself 'the Sign' of the way, according to the traditional iconography of East and West.

970

512

2619

2675 Beginning with Mary's unique co–operation with the working of the Holy Spirit, the Churches developed their prayer to the holy Mother of God, centring it on the person of Christ manifested in his mysteries. In countless hymns and antiphons expressing this prayer, two movements usually alternate with one another: the first 'magnifies' the Lord for the 'great things' he did for his lowly servant and through her for all human beings;[29] the second entrusts the supplications and praises of the children of God to the Mother of Jesus, because she now knows the humanity which, in her, the Son of God espoused.

2676 This twofold movement of prayer to Mary has found a privileged expression in the *Ave Maria*:

722

Hail Mary [or Rejoice, Mary]: the greeting of the angel Gabriel opens this prayer. It is God himself who, through his angel as intermediary, greets Mary. Our prayer dares to take up this greeting to Mary with the regard God had for the lowliness of his humble servant and to exult in the joy he finds in her.[30]

490

Full of grace, the Lord is with thee: These two phrases of the angel's greeting shed light on one another. Mary is full of grace because the Lord is with her. The grace with which she is filled is the presence of him who is the source of all grace. 'Rejoice ... O Daughter of Jerusalem ... the LORD your God is in your midst.'[31] Mary, in whom the Lord himself has just made his dwelling, is the daughter of Zion in person, the ark of the covenant, the place where the glory of the Lord dwells. She is 'the dwelling of God ... with men.'[32] Full of grace, Mary is wholly given over to him who has come to dwell in her and whom she is about to give to the world.

435

Blessed art thou among women and blessed is the fruit of thy womb, Jesus. After the angel's greeting, we make Elizabeth's greeting our own. 'Filled with the Holy Spirit', Elizabeth is the first in the long succession of generations who have called Mary 'blessed.'[33] 'Blessed is she who believed ...'[34] Mary is 'blessed among women' because she believed in the fulfilment of the Lord's word. Abraham, because of his faith, became a blessing for all the nations of the earth.[35] Mary, because of her faith, became the mother of believers, through whom all nations of the earth receive him who is God's own blessing: Jesus, the 'fruit of thy womb.'

146

---

28 *LG* 62.
29 Cf. *Lk* 1:46–55.
30 Cf. *Lk* 1:48; *Zeph* 3:17b.
31 *Zeph* 3:14, 17a.

32 *Rev* 21:3.
33 *Lk* 1:41, 48.
34 *Lk* 1:45.
35 Cf. *Gen* 12:3.

2677 *Holy Mary, Mother of God*: With Elizabeth we marvel, 'And why is   495
this granted me, that the mother of my Lord should come to me?' [36] Because
she gives us Jesus, her son, Mary is Mother of God and our mother; we can
entrust all our cares and petitions to her: she prays for us as she prayed for
herself: 'Let it be to me according to your word.' [37] By entrusting ourselves
to her prayer, we abandon ourselves to the will of God together with her:
'Thy will be done.'

Pray for us sinners, now and at the hour of our death: By asking Mary to
pray for us, we acknowledge ourselves to be poor sinners and we address
ourselves to the 'Mother of Mercy', the All-Holy One. We give ourselves
over to her now, in the Today of our lives. And our trust broadens further,
already at the present moment, to surrender 'the hour of our death' wholly   1020
to her care. May she be there as she was at her son's death on the cross.
May she welcome us as our mother at the hour of our passing[38] to lead us
to her son, Jesus, in paradise.

2678 Medieval piety in the West developed the prayer of the rosary   971, 1674
as a popular substitute for the Liturgy of the Hours. In the East, the
litany called the *Akathistos* and the *Paraclesis* remained closer to the
choral office in the Byzantine churches, while the Armenian, Coptic
and Syriac traditions preferred popular hymns and songs to the Mother
of God. But in the *Ave Maria*, the *theotokia*, the hymns of St Ephrem
or St Gregory of Narek, the tradition of prayer isbasically the same.

2679 Mary is the perfect *Orans* [pray-er], a figure of the Church.   967
When we pray to her, we are adhering with her to the plan of the
Father, who sends his Son to save all men. Like the beloved disciple
we welcome Jesus' mother into our homes,[39] for she has become the
mother of all the living. We can pray with and to her. The prayer of
the Church is sustained by the prayer of Mary and united with it in   972
hope.[40]

IN BRIEF

2680 *Prayer is primarily addressed to the Father; it can also be
directed toward Jesus, particularly by the invocation of his holy
name: 'Lord Jesus Christ, Son of God, have mercy on us sinners.'*

2681 *'No one can say "Jesus is Lord", except by the Holy Spirit.'
(1 Cor 12,3) The Church invites us to invoke the Holy Spirit as
the interior Teacher of Christian prayer.*

---

36 *Lk* 1:43.   39 Cf. *Jn* 19:27.
37 *Lk* 1:38.   40 Cf. *LG* 68–69.
38 Cf. *Jn* 19:27.

> 2682 Because of Mary's singular co–operation with the action of the Holy Spirit, the Church loves to pray in communion with the Virgin Mary, to magnify with her the great things the Lord has done for her and to entrust supplications and praises to her.

ARTICLE 3
Guides for Prayer

A cloud of witnesses

956

2683 The witnesses who have preceded us into the kingdom,[41] especially those whom the Church recognises as saints, share in the living tradition of prayer by the example of their lives, the transmission of their writings and their prayer today. They contemplate God, praise him and constantly care for those whom they have left on earth. When they entered into the joy of their Master, they were 'put in charge of many things.'[42] Their intercession is their most exalted service to God's plan. We can and should ask them to intercede for us and for the whole world.

917

919
1202

2684 In the communion of saints, many and varied *spiritualities* have been developed throughout the history of the Churches. The personal charism of some witnesses to God's love for men has been handed on, like 'the spirit' of Elijah to Elisha and John the Baptist, so that their followers may have a share in this spirit.[43] A distinct spirituality can also arise at the point of convergence of liturgical and theological currents, bearing witness to the integration of the faith into a particular human environment and its history. The different schools of Christian spirituality share in the living tradition of prayer and are essential guides for the faithful. In their rich diversity they are refractions of the one pure light of the Holy Spirit.

> The Spirit is truly the dwelling of the saints and the saints are for the Spirit a place where he dwells as in his own home, since they offer themselves as a dwelling place for God and are called his temple.[44]

Servants of prayer

1657

2685 The *Christian family* is the first place of education in prayer. Based on the sacrament of marriage, the family is the 'domestic church' where God's children learn to pray 'as the Church', and to persevere in prayer. For young children in particular, daily family

---

41 Cf. *Heb* 12:1.
42 Cf. *Mt* 25:21.
43 Cf. *2 Kings* 2:9; *Lk* 1:1; PC 2.

44 St Basil, *De Spiritu Sancto*, 26, 62: PG 32, 184.

prayer is the first witness of the Church's living memory as awakened patiently by the Holy Spirit.

2686 *Ordained ministers* are also responsible for the formation in prayer of their brothers and sisters in Christ. Servants of the Good Shepherd, they are ordained to lead the People of God to the living waters of prayer: the Word of God, the liturgy, the theologal life [the life of faith, hope and charity], and the Today of God in concrete situations.[45]

1547

2687 Many *religious* have consecrated their whole lives to prayer. Hermits, monks and nuns since the time of the desert fathers have devoted their time to praising God and interceding for his people. The consecrated life cannot be sustained or spread without prayer; it is one of the living sources of contemplation and the spiritual life of the Church.

916

2688 The *catechesis* of children, young people and adults aims at teaching them to meditate on The Word of God in personal prayer, practising it in liturgical prayer and internalizing it at all times in order to bear fruit in a new life. Catechesis is also a time for the discernment and education of popular piety.[46] The memorization of basic prayers offers an essential support to the life of prayer, but it is important to help learners savour their meaning.

1674

2689 *Prayer groups*, indeed 'schools of prayer', are today one of the signs and one of the driving forces of renewal of prayer in the Church, provided they drink from authentic wellsprings of Christian prayer. Concern for ecclesial communion is a sign of true prayer in the Church.

2690 The Holy Spirit gives to certain of the faithful the gifts of wisdom, faith and discernment for the sake of this common good which is prayer (*spiritual direction*). Men and women so endowed are true servants of the living tradition of prayer.

> According to St John of the Cross, the person wishing to advance toward perfection should 'take care into whose hands he entrusts himself, for as the master is, so will the disciple be, and as the father is so will be the son.' And further: 'In addition to being learned and discreet a director should be experienced ... If the spiritual director has no experience of the spiritual life, he will be incapable of leading into it the souls whom God is calling to it, and he will not even understand them.'[47]

---

45 Cf. *PO* 4–6.
46 Cf. *CT* 54.
47 St John of the Cross, *The Living Flame of Love*, stanza 3, 30, in *The Collected Works of St John of the Cross*, eds K. Kavanaugh OCD and O. Rodriguez OCD (Washington DC: Institute of Carmelite Studies, 1979), 621.

Places favourable for prayer

1181
2179
1379

2691 The church, the house of God, is the proper place for the liturgical prayer of the parish community. It is also the privileged place for adoration of the real presence of Christ in the Blessed Sacrament. The choice of a favourable place is not a matter of indifference for true prayer.

- For personal prayer, this can be a 'prayer corner' with the sacred Scriptures and icons, in order to be there, in secret, before our Father.[48] In a Christian family, this kind of little oratory fosters prayer in common.

1175

- In regions where monasteries exist, the vocation of these communities is to further the participation of the faithful in the Liturgy of the Hours and to provide necessary solitude for more intense personal prayer.[49]

1674

- Pilgrimages evoke our earthly journey toward heaven and are traditionally very special occasions for renewal in prayer. For pilgrims seeking living water, shrines are special places for living the forms of Christian prayer 'in Church.'

IN BRIEF

2692 *In prayer, the pilgrim Church is associated with that of the saints, whose intercession she asks.*

2693 *The different schools of Christian spirituality share in the living tradition of prayer and are precious guides for the spiritual life.*

2694 *The Christian family is the first place for education in prayer.*

2695 *Ordained ministers, the consecrated life, catechesis, prayer groups and 'spiritual direction' ensure assistance within the Church in the practice of prayer.*

2696 *The most appropriate places for prayer are personal or family oratories, monasteries, places of pilgrimage, and above all the church, which is the proper place for liturgical prayer for the parish community and the privileged place for Eucharistic adoration.*

---

48 Cf. *Mt* 6:6.   49 Cf. *PC 7.*

CHAPTER THREE
THE LIFE OF PRAYER

2697 Prayer is the life of the new heart. It ought to animate us at every moment. But we tend to forget him who is our life and our all. This is why the Fathers of the spiritual life in the Deuteronomic and prophetic traditions insist that prayer is a remembrance of God often awakened by the memory of the heart: 'We must remember God more often than we draw breath.'[1] But we cannot pray 'at all times' if we do not pray at specific times, consciously willing it. These are the special times of Christian prayer, both in intensity and duration.   1099

2698 The Tradition of the Church proposes to the faithful certain rhythms of praying intended to nourish continual prayer. Some are daily, such as morning and evening prayer, grace before and after meals, the Liturgy of the Hours. Sundays, centred on the Eucharist, are kept holy primarily by prayer. The cycle of the liturgical year and its great feasts are also basic rhythms of the Christian's life of prayer.   1168 1174 2177

2699 The Lord leads all persons by paths and in ways pleasing to him, and each believer responds according to his heart's resolve and the personal expressions of his prayer. However, Christian tradition has retained three major expressions of prayer: vocal, meditative and contemplative. They have one basic trait in common: composure of heart. This vigilance in keeping the Word and dwelling in the presence of God makes these three expressions intense times in the life of prayer.   2563

ARTICLE 1
Expressions of Prayer

I. Vocal Prayer

2700 Through his Word, God speaks to man. By words, mental or vocal, our prayer takes flesh. Yet it is most important that the heart should be present to him to whom we are speaking in prayer: 'Whether or not our prayer is heard depends not on the number of words, but on the fervour of our souls.'[2]   1176

2701 Vocal prayer is an essential element of the Christian life. To his disciples, drawn by their Master's silent prayer, Jesus teaches a vocal prayer, the *Our Father*. He not only prayed aloud the liturgical prayers of the synagogue but, as the Gospels show, he raised his   2603

---

1 St Gregory of Nazianzus, *Oratio* 27, 4: PG 36, 16.

2 St John Chrysostom, *Ecloga de oratione* 2: PG 63, 585.

612

voice to express his personal prayer, from exultant blessing of the Father to the agony of Gesthemani.[3]

1146

2702 The need to involve the senses in interior prayer corresponds to a requirement of our human nature. We are body and spirit, and we experience the need to translate our feelings externally. We must pray with our whole being to give all power possible to our supplication.

2703 This need also corresponds to a divine requirement. God seeks worshippers in Spirit and in Truth, and consequently living prayer that rises from the depths of the soul. He also wants the external expression that associates the body with interior prayer, for it renders

2097

him that perfect homage which is his due.

2704 Because it is external and so thoroughly human, vocal prayer is the form of prayer most readily accessible to groups. Even interior prayer, however, cannot neglect vocal prayer. Prayer is internalized to the extent that we become aware of him 'to whom we speak.'[4] Thus vocal prayer becomes an initial form of contemplative prayer.

II. Meditation

158

2705 Meditation is above all a quest. The mind seeks to understand the why and how of the Christian life, in order to adhere and respond to what the Lord is asking. The required attentiveness is difficult to sustain. We are usually helped by books, and Christians

127

do not want for them: the Sacred Scriptures, particularly the Gospels, holy icons, liturgical texts of the day or season, writings of the spiritual fathers, works of spirituality, the great book of creation, and that of history – the page on which the 'today' of God is written.

2706 To meditate on what we read helps us to make it our own by confronting it with ourselves. Here, another book is opened: the book of life. We pass from thoughts to reality. To the extent that we are humble and faithful, we discover in meditation the movements that stir the heart and we are able to discern them. It is a question of acting truthfully in order to come into the light: 'Lord, what do you want me to do?'

2690

2707 There are as many and varied methods of meditation as there are spiritual masters. Christians owe it to themselves to develop the desire to meditate regularly, lest they come to resemble the three

---

3 Cf. *Mt* 11:25–26; *Mk* 14:36.

4 St Teresa of Jesus, *The Way of Perfection* 26, 9 in *The Collected Works of St. Teresa of Avila,* tr. K. Kavanaugh OCD and O. Rodriguez OCD (Washington DC: Institute of Carmelite Studies, 1980), II, 136.

first kinds of soil in the parable of the sower.[5] But a method is only a guide; the important thing is to advance, with the Holy Spirit, along the one way of prayer: Christ Jesus.

2664

2708 Meditation engages thought, imagination, emotion and desire. This mobilisation of faculties is necessary in order to deepen our convictions of faith, prompt the conversion of our heart and strengthen our will to follow Christ. Christian prayer tries above all to meditate on the mysteries of Christ, as in *lectio divina* or the rosary. This form of prayerful reflection is of great value, but Christian prayer should go further: to the knowledge of the love of the Lord Jesus, to union with him.

516
2678

III. Contemplative Prayer

2709 What is contemplative prayer? St Teresa answers: 'Contemplative prayer [*oración mental*] in my opinion is nothing else than a close sharing between friends; it means taking time frequently to be alone with him who we know loves us.'[6]

2562-2564

Contemplative prayer seeks him 'whom my soul loves.'[7] It is Jesus, and in him, the Father. We seek him, because to desire him is always the beginning of love, and we seek him in that pure faith which causes us to be born of him and to live in him. In this inner prayer we can still meditate, but our attention is fixed on the Lord himself.

2710 The choice of the *time and duration of the prayer* arises from a determined will, revealing the secrets of the heart. One does not undertake contemplative prayer only when one has the time: one makes time for the Lord, with the firm determination not to give up, no matter what trials and dryness one may encounter. One cannot always meditate, but one can always enter into inner prayer, independently of the conditions of health, work or emotional state. The heart is the place of this quest and encounter, in poverty and in faith.

2726

2711 *Entering into contemplative prayer* is like entering into the Eucharistic liturgy: we 'gather up' the heart, recollect our whole being under the prompting of the Holy Spirit, abide in the dwelling place of the Lord which we are, awaken our faith in order to enter into the presence of him who awaits us. We let our masks fall and turn our hearts back to the Lord who loves us, so as to hand ourselves over to him as an offering to be purified and transformed.

1348

2100

---

5 Cf. *Mk* 4:4–7, 15–19.
6 St Teresa of Jesus, *The Book of Her Life*, 8,5 in *The Collected Works of St Teresa of Avila*, tr. K.Kavanaugh

OCD and O. Rodriguez OCD (Washington DC: Institute of Carmelite Studies, 1976), I, 67.
7 *Song* 1:7; cf. 3:1-4.

2822

2712 Contemplative prayer is the prayer of the child of God, of the forgiven sinner who agrees to welcome the love by which he is loved and who wants to respond to it by loving even more.[8] But he knows that the love he is returning is poured out by the Spirit in his heart, for everything is grace from God. Contemplative prayer is the poor and humble surrender to the loving will of the Father in ever deeper union with his beloved Son.

2559

2713 Contemplative prayer is the simplest expression of the mystery of prayer. It is a *gift*, a grace; it can be accepted only in humility and poverty. Contemplative prayer is a *covenant* relationship established by God within our hearts.[9] Contemplative prayer is a *communion* in which the Holy Trinity conforms man, the image of God, 'to his likeness.'

2714 Contemplative prayer is also the pre-eminently *intense time* of prayer. In it the Father strengthens our inner being with power through his Spirit 'that Christ may dwell in [our] hearts through faith' and we may be 'grounded in love.'[10]

521

2715 Contemplation is a *gaze* of faith, fixed on Jesus. 'I look at him and he looks at me': this is what a certain peasant of Ars used to say to his holy curé about his prayer before the tabernacle. This focus on Jesus is a renunciation of self. His gaze purifies our heart; the light of the countenance of Jesus illumines the eyes of our heart and teaches us to see everything in the light of his truth and his compassion for all men. Contemplation also turns its gaze on the mysteries of the life of Christ. Thus it learns the 'interior knowledge of our Lord', the more to love him and follow him.[11]

494

2716 Contemplative prayer is *hearing* the Word of God. Far from being passive, such attentiveness is the obedience of faith, the unconditional acceptance of a servant and the loving commitment of a child. It participates in the 'Yes' of the Son become servant and the *Fiat* of God's lowly handmaid.

533

498

2717 Contemplative prayer is *silence*, the 'symbol of the world to come'[12] or 'silent love'.[13] Words in this kind of prayer are not speeches; they are like kindling that feeds the fire of love. In this silence, unbearable to the 'outer' man, the Father speaks to us his incarnate Word, who suffered, died and rose; in this silence the Spirit of adoption enables us to share in the prayer of Jesus.

---

8 Cf. *Lk* 7:36–50; 19:1–10.
9 Cf. *Jer* 31:33.
10 *Eph* 3:16–17.
11 Cf. St Ignatius of Loyola, *Spiritual Exercises*, 104.
12 Cf. St Isaac of Nineveh, *Tract. myst.* 66.

13 St John of the Cross, *Maxims and Counsels*, 53 in *The Collected Works of St John of the Cross*, tr. K. Kavanaugh OCD and O. Rodriguez OCD (Washington DC: Institute of Carmelite Studies, 1979), 678.

2718 Contemplative prayer is a union with the prayer of Christ insofar as it makes us participate in his mystery. The mystery of Christ is celebrated by the Church in the Eucharist, and the Holy Spirit makes it come alive in contemplative prayer so that our charity will manifest it in our acts.

2719 Contemplative prayer is a communion of love bearing Life for the multitude, to the extent that it consents to abide in the night of faith. The Paschal night of the Resurrection passes through the night of the agony and the tomb – the three intense moments of the Hour of Jesus which his Spirit (and not 'the flesh [which] is weak') brings to life in prayer. We must be willing to 'keep watch-with [him] one hour.'[14]

165

2730

IN BRIEF

2720 *The Church invites the faithful to regular prayer: daily prayers, the Liturgy of the Hours, Sunday Eucharist, the feasts of the liturgical year.*

2721 *The Christian tradition comprises three major expressions of the life of prayer: vocal prayer, meditation and contemplative prayer. They have in common the recollection of the heart.*

2722 *Vocal prayer, founded on the union of body and soul in human nature, associates the body with the interior prayer of the heart, following Christ's example of praying to his Father and teaching the Our Father to his disciples.*

2723 *Meditation is a prayerful quest engaging thought, imagination, emotion and desire. Its goal is to make our own in faith the subject considered, by confronting it with the reality of our own life.*

2724 *Contemplative prayer is the simple expression of the mystery of prayer. It is a gaze of faith fixed on Jesus, an attentiveness to the Word of God, a silent love. It achieves real union with the prayer of Christ to the extent that it makes us share in his mystery.*

ARTICLE 2
The Battle of Prayer

2725 Prayer is both a gift of grace and a determined response on our part. It always presupposes effort. The great figures of prayer of the Old Covenant before Christ, as well as the Mother of God, the saints, and he himself, all teach us this: prayer is a battle. Against

2612, 409

---

14 Cf. *Mt* 26:40.

whom? Against ourselves and against the wiles of the tempter who does all he can to turn man away from prayer, away from union with God. We pray as we live, because we live as we pray. If we do not want to act habitually according to the Spirit of Christ, neither can we pray habitually in his name. The 'spiritual battle' of the Christian's new life is inseparable from the battle of prayer.

2015

I. Objections to Prayer

2726 In the battle of prayer, we must face in ourselves and around us *erroneous notions of prayer*. Some people view prayer as a simple psychological activity, others as an effort of concentration to reach a mental void. Still others reduce prayer to ritual words and postures. Many Christians unconsciously regard prayer as an occupation that is incompatible with all the other things they have to do: they 'don't have the time'. Those who seek God by prayer are quickly discouraged because they do not know that prayer comes also from the Holy Spirit and not from themselves alone.

2710

2727 We must also face the fact that certain attitudes deriving from the *mentality* of 'this present world' can penetrate our lives if we are not vigilant. For example, some would have it that only that is true which can be verified by reason and science; yet prayer is a mystery that overflows both our conscious and unconscious lives. Others overly prize production and profit; thus prayer, being unproductive, is useless. Still others exalt sensuality and comfort as the criteria of the true, the good and the beautiful; whereas prayer, the 'love of beauty' [*philokalia*], is caught up in the glory of the living and true God. Finally, some see prayer as a flight from the world in reaction against activism; but in fact, Christian prayer is neither an escape from reality nor a divorce from life.

37

2500

2728 Finally, our battle has to confront what we experience as *failure in prayer*: discouragement during periods of dryness; sadness that, because we have 'great possessions',[15] we have not given all to the Lord; disappointment over not being heard according to our own will; wounded pride, stiffened by the indignity that is ours as sinners; our resistance to the idea that prayer is a free and unmerited gift; and so forth. The conclusion is always the same: what good does it do to pray? To overcome these obstacles, we must battle to gain humility, trust and perseverance.

II. Humble Vigilance of Heart
Facing difficulties in prayer

2729 The habitual difficulty in prayer is *distraction*. It can affect words and their meaning in vocal prayer; it can concern, more pro-

---

15 Cf. *Mk* 10:22.

foundly, him to whom we are praying, in vocal prayer (liturgical or personal), meditation and contemplative prayer. To set about hunting down distractions would be to fall into their trap, when all that is necessary is to turn back to our heart: for a distraction reveals to us what we are attached to, and this humble awareness before the Lord should awaken our preferential love for him and lead us resolutely to offer him our heart to be purified. Therein lies the battle, the choice of which master to serve.[16]

2711

2730 In positive terms, the battle against the possessive and dominating self requires *vigilance*, sobriety of heart. When Jesus insists on vigilance, he always relates it to himself, to his coming on the last day and every day: *today*. The bridegroom comes in the middle of the night; the light that must not be extinguished is that of faith: ' "Come", my heart says, "seek his face!" '[17]

2659

2731 Another difficulty, especially for those who sincerely want to pray, is *dryness*. Dryness belongs to contemplative prayer when the heart is separated from God, with no taste for thoughts, memories and feelings, even spiritual ones. This is the moment of sheer faith clinging faithfully to Jesus in his agony and in his tomb. 'Unless a grain of wheat falls into the earth and dies, it remains alone; but if it dies, it bears much fruit.'[18] If dryness is due to the lack of roots, because the word has fallen on rocky soil, the battle requires conversion.[19]

1426

Facing temptations in prayer

2732 The most common yet most hidden temptation is our *lack of faith*. It expresses itself less by declared incredulity than by our actual preferences. When we begin to pray, a thousand labours or cares thought to be urgent vie for priority; once again, it is the moment of truth for the heart: what is its real love? Sometimes we turn to the Lord as a last resort, but do we really believe he is? Sometimes we enlist the Lord as an ally, but our heart remains presumptuous. In each case, our lack of faith reveals that we do not yet share in the disposition of a humble heart: 'Apart from me, you can do *nothing*.'[20]

2609, 2089

2092
2074

2733 Another temptation, to which presumption opens the gate, is *acedia*. The spiritual writers understand by this a form of depression due to lax ascetical practice, decreasing vigilance, carelessness of heart. 'The spirit indeed is willing, but the flesh is weak.'[21] The greater the height, the harder the fall. Painful as discouragement is,

2094

---

16 Cf. *Mt* 6:21, 24.
17 *Ps* 27:8.
18 *Jn* 12:24.

19 Cf. *Lk* 8:6, 13.
20 *Jn* 15:5.
21 *Mt* 26:41.

2559   it is the reverse of presumption. The humble are not surprised by
their distress; it leads them to trust more, to hold fast in constancy.

III. Filial Trust

2734 Filial trust is tested — it proves itself — in tribulation.[22] The
2629   principal difficulty concerns the *prayer of petition*, for oneself or for
others in intercession. Some even stop praying because they think
their petition is not heard. Here two questions should be asked:
Why do we think our petition has not been heard? How is our
prayer heard, how is it 'efficacious'?

Why do we complain of not being heard?

2735   In the first place, we ought to be astonished by this fact: when
we praise God or give him thanks for his benefits in general, we are
not particularly concerned whether or not our prayer is acceptable
to him. On the other hand, we demand to see the results of our
2779   petitions. What is the image of God that motivates our prayer: an
instrument to be used? or the Father of our Lord Jesus Christ?

2559   2736 Are we convinced that 'we do not know how to pray as we
ought'?[23] Are we asking God for 'what is good for us'? Our Father
1730   knows what we need before we ask him,[24] but he awaits our petition
because the dignity of his children lies in their freedom. We must
pray, then, with his Spirit of freedom, to be able truly to know what
he wants.[25]

2737 'You ask and do not receive, because you ask wrongly, to
spend it on your passions.'[26] If we ask with a divided heart, we are
'adulterers';[27] God cannot answer us, for he desires our well-being,
our life. 'Or do you suppose that it is in vain that the scripture says,
"He yearns jealously over the spirit which he has made to dwell in
us"?'[28] That our God is 'jealous' for us is the sign of how true his
love is. If we enter into the desire of his Spirit we shall be heard.

> Do not be troubled if you do not immediately receive from God what
> you ask him; for he desires to do something even greater for you, while
> you cling to him in prayer.[29]

> God wills that our desire should be exercised in prayer, that we may be
> able to receive what he is prepared to give.[30]

---

22 Cf. *Rom* 5:3–5.
23 *Rom* 8:26.
24 Cf. *Mt* 6:8.
25 Cf. *Rom* 8:27.
26 *Jas* 4:3; cf. the whole context:
    Jas 4:1–10; 1:5–8; 5:16.
27 *Jas* 4:4.
28 *Jas* 4:5.
29 Evagrius Ponticus, *De oratione* 34:
    PG 79, 1173.
30 St Augustine, *Ep.* 130, 8, 17:
    PL 33, 500.

How is our prayer efficacious?

2738 The revelation of prayer in the economy of salvation teaches us that faith rests on God's action in history. Our filial trust is enkindled by his supreme act: the Passion and Resurrection of his Son. Christian prayer is cooperation with his providence, his plan of love for men.

2568

307

2739 For St Paul, this trust is bold, founded on the prayer of the Spirit in us and on the faithful love of the Father who has given us his only Son.[31] Transformation of the praying heart is the first response to our petition.

2778

2740 The prayer of Jesus makes Christian prayer an efficacious petition. He is its model, he prays in us and with us. Since the heart of the Son seeks only what pleases the Father, how could the prayer of the children of adoption be centred on the gifts rather than the Giver?

2604

2741 Jesus also prays for us – in our place and on our behalf. All our petitions were gathered up, once for all, in his cry on the Cross and, in his Resurrection, heard by the Father. This is why he never ceases to intercede for us with the Father.[32] If our prayer is resolutely united with that of Jesus, in trust and boldness as children, we obtain all that we ask in his name, even more than any particular thing: the Holy Spirit himself, who contains all gifts.

2606

2614

IV. Persevering in Love

2742 'Pray constantly ... always and for everything giving thanks in the name of our Lord Jesus Christ to God the Father.'[33] St Paul adds, 'Pray at all times in the Spirit, with all prayer and supplication. To that end keep alert with all perseverance making supplication for all the saints.'[34] For 'we have not been commanded to work, to keep watch and to fast constantly, but it has been laid down that we are to pray without ceasing.'[35] This tireless fervour can come only from love. Against our dullness and laziness, the battle of prayer is that of humble, trusting and persevering *love*. This love opens our hearts to three enlightening and life-giving facts of faith about prayer.

2098

162

2743 *It is always possible to pray*: The time of the Christian is that of the risen Christ who is with us always, no matter what tempests may arise.[36] Our time is in the hands of God:

---

31 Cf. *Rom* 10:12–13; 8:26–39.
32 Cf. *Heb* 5:7; 7:25; 9:24.
33 1 *Th* 5:17; *Eph* 5:20.
34 *Eph* 6:18.

35 Evagrius Ponticus, *Pract.* 49:
    PG 40, 1245C.
36 Cf. *Mt* 28:20; *Lk* 8:24.

> It is possible to offer fervent prayer even while walking in public or strolling alone, or seated in your shop, ... while buying or selling, ... or even while cooking.[37]

2744 *Prayer is a vital necessity.* Proof from the contrary is no less convincing: if we do not allow the Spirit to lead us, we fall back into the slavery of sin.[38] How can the Holy Spirit be our life if our heart is far from him?

> Nothing is equal to prayer; for what is impossible it makes possible, what is difficult, easy ... For it is impossible, utterly impossible, for the man who prays eagerly and invokes God ceaselessly ever to sin.[39]

> Those who pray are certainly saved; those who do not pray are certainly damned.[40]

2660

2745 Prayer and *Christian life* are *inseparable,* for they concern the same love and the same renunciation, proceeding from love; the same filial and loving conformity with the Father's plan of love; the same transforming union in the Holy Spirit who conforms us more and more to Christ Jesus; the same love for all men, the love with which Jesus has loved us. 'Whatever you ask the Father in my name, he [will] give it to you. This I command you, to love one another.'[41]

> He 'prays without ceasing' who unites prayer to works and good works to prayer. Only in this way can we consider as realisable the principle of praying without ceasing.[42]

ARTICLE 3
The Prayer of the Hour of Jesus

1085

2746 When 'his hour' came, Jesus prayed to the Father.[43] His prayer, the longest transmitted by the Gospel, embraces the whole economy of creation and salvation, as well as his death and Resurrection. The prayer of the Hour of Jesus always remains his own, just as his Passover 'once for all' remains ever present in the liturgy of his Church.

2747 Christian tradition rightly calls this prayer the 'priestly' prayer of Jesus. It is the prayer of our high priest, inseparable from his sacrifice, from his passing over (Passover) to the Father to whom he is wholly 'consecrated.'[44]

---

37 St John Chrysostom, *Ecloga de oratione* 2: PG 63, 585.
38 Cf. *Gal* 5:16–25.
39 St John Chrysostom, *De Anna* 4, 5: PG 54, 666.
40 St Alphonsus Liguori, *Del gran mezzo della preghiera.*
41 *Jn* 15:16–17 .
42 Origen, *De orat.* 12: PG 11, 452C.
43 Cf. *Jn* 17.
44 Cf. *Jn* 17:11, 13, 19.

2748 In this Paschal and sacrificial prayer, everything is recapitulated in Christ:[45] God and the world; the Word and the flesh; eternal life and time; the love that hands itself over and the sin that betrays it; the disciples present and those who will believe in him by their word; humiliation and glory. It is the prayer of unity.

518

820

2749 Jesus fulfilled the work of the Father completely; his prayer, like his sacrifice, extends until the end of time. The prayer of this hour fills the end-times and carries them toward their consummation. Jesus, the Son to whom the Father has given all things, has given himself wholly back to the Father, yet expresses himself with a sovereign freedom[46] by virtue of the power the Father has given him over all flesh. The Son, who made himself Servant, is Lord, the *Pantocrator*. Our high priest who prays for us is also the one who prays in us and the God who hears our prayer.

2616

2750 By entering into the holy name of the Lord Jesus we can accept, from within, the prayer he teaches us: 'Our Father!' His priestly prayer fulfils, from within, the great petitions of the Lord's Prayer: concern for the Father's name;[47] passionate zeal for his kingdom (glory);[48] the accomplishment of the will of the Father, of his plan of salvation;[49] and deliverance from evil.[50]

2815

2751 Finally, in this prayer Jesus reveals and gives to us the 'knowledge', inseparably one, of the Father and of the Son,[51] which is the very mystery of the life of prayer.

240

IN BRIEF

2752 Prayer presupposes an effort, a fight against ourselves and the wiles of the Tempter. The battle of prayer is inseparable from the necessary 'spiritual battle' to act habitually according to the Spirit of Christ: we pray as we live, because we live as we pray.

2753 In the battle of prayer we must confront erroneous conceptions of prayer, various currents of thought and our own experience of failure. We must respond with humility, trust and perseverance to these temptations which cast doubt on the usefulness or even the possibility of prayer.

2754 The principal difficulties in the practice of prayer are distraction and dryness. The remedy lies in faith, conversion, and vigilance of heart.

---

45 Cf. *Eph* 1:10.
46 Cf. *Jn* 17:11, 13, 19, 24.
47 Cf. *Jn* 17:6, 11, 12, 26.
48 Cf. *Jn* 17:1, 5, 10, 24, 23-26.
49 Cf. *Jn* 17:2, 4, 6, 9, 11, 12, 24.
50 Cf. *Jn* 17:15.
51 Cf. *Jn* 17:3, 6–10, 25.

2755 Two frequent temptations threaten prayer: lack of faith, and acedia – a form of depression stemming from lax ascetical practice that leads to discouragement.

2756 Filial trust is put to the test when we feel that our prayer is not always heard. The Gospel invites us to ask ourselves about the conformity of our prayer to the desire of the Spirit.

2757 'Pray constantly.' (1 Th 5:17) It is always possible to pray. It is even a vital necessity. Prayer and Christian life are inseparable.

2758 The prayer of the hour of Jesus, rightly called the 'priestly prayer' (cf. Jn 17), sums up the whole economy of creation and salvation. It fulfils the great petitions of the Our Father.

PART TWO
THE LORD'S PRAYER: 'OUR FATHER!'

2759 Jesus 'was praying at a certain place, and when he ceased, one of his disciples said to him, "Lord, teach us to pray, as John taught his disciples".' [1] In response to this request the Lord entrusts to his disciples and to his Church the fundamental Christian prayer. St Luke presents a brief text of five petitions,[2] while St. Matthew gives a more developed version of seven petitions.[3] The liturgical tradition of the Church has retained St Matthew's text:

Our Father who art in heaven,
hallowed be thy name.
Thy kingdom come.
Thy will be done on earth, as it is in heaven.
Give us this day our daily bread,
and forgive us our trespasses,
as we forgive those who trespass against us,
and lead us not into temptation,
but deliver us from evil.

2855

2760 Very early on, liturgical usage concluded the Lord's Prayer with a doxology. In the *Didache*, we find, 'For yours are the power and the glory for ever.' [4] The *Apostolic Constitutions* add to the beginning: 'the king-

---

1 *Lk* 11:1.
2 Cf. *Lk* 11:2–4.
3 Cf. *Mt* 6:9–13.
4 *Didache* 8, 2: SCh 248, 174.

dom', and this is the formula retained to our day in ecumenical prayer.[5]
The Byzantine tradition adds after 'the glory' the words 'Father, Son, and
Holy Spirit.' The *Roman Missal* develops the last petition in the explicit
perspective of 'awaiting our blessed hope' and of the Second Coming of our
Lord Jesus Christ.[6] Then comes the assembly's acclamation, or the repeti-
tion of the doxology from the *Apostolic Constitutions.*

2854

ARTICLE 1
'The Summary of the Whole Gospel'

2761 The Lord's Prayer 'is truly the summary of the whole gospel.'
[7] 'Since the Lord ... after handing over the practice of prayer, said
elsewhere, "Ask and you will receive", and since everyone has petitions which are peculiar to his circumstances, the regular and appropriate prayer [the Lord's Prayer] is said first, as the foundation of
further desires.'[8]

I. At the Centre of the Scriptures

2762 After showing how the Psalms are the principal food of Christian prayer and flow together in the petitions of the *Our Father*,
St Augustine concludes:

> Run through all the words of the holy prayers [in Scripture], and I do
> not think that you will find anything in them that is not contained and
> included in the Lord's Prayer.[9]

2763 All the Scriptures – the Law, the Prophets and the Psalms –
are fulfilled in Christ.[10] The Gospel is this 'Good News'. Its first
proclamation is summarized by St Matthew in the Sermon on the
Mount;[11] the prayer to our Father is at the centre of this proclamation. It is in this context that each petition bequeathed to us by
the Lord is illuminated:

102

> The Lord's Prayer is the most perfect of prayers ... In it we ask, not
> only for all the things we can rightly desire, but also in the sequence
> that they should be desired. This prayer not only teaches us to ask for
> things, but also in what order we should desire them.[12]

2541

2764 The Sermon on the Mount is teaching for life, the *Our Father*
is a prayer; but in both the one and the other the Spirit of the Lord
gives new form to our desires, those inner movements that animate

1965

---

5 *Const. App.* 7, 24, 1: PG 1, 1016.
6 *Titus* 2:13; cf. *Roman Missal* 22,
   Embolism after the Lord's Prayer.
7 Tertullian, *De orat.* 1: PL 1, 1155.
8 Tertullian, *De orat.* 10: PL 1, 1165;
   cf. *Lk* 11:9.

9 St Augustine, *Ep.* 130, 12, 22:
   PL 33, 503.
10 Cf. *Lk* 24:44.
11 Cf. *Mt* 5–7.
12 St Thomas Aquinas, *STh.* II–II,
   83, 9.

1969

our lives. Jesus teaches us this new life by his words; he teaches us to ask for it by our prayer. The rightness of our life in him will depend on the rightness of our prayer.

II. 'The Lord's Prayer'

2701

2765 The traditional expression 'the Lord's Prayer' – *oratio Dominica* – means that the prayer to our Father is taught and given to us by the Lord Jesus. The prayer that comes to us from Jesus is truly unique: it is 'of the Lord'. On the one hand, in the words of this prayer the only Son gives us the words the Father gave him:[13] he is the master of our prayer. On the other, as Word incarnate, he knows in his human heart the needs of his human brothers and sisters and reveals them to us: he is the model of our prayer.

2766 But Jesus does not give us a formula to repeat mechanically.[14] As in every vocal prayer, it is through the Word of God that the Holy Spirit teaches the children of God to pray to their Father. Jesus not only gives us the words of our filial prayer; at the same time he gives us the Spirit by whom these words become in us 'spirit and life'.[15] Even more, the proof and possibility of our filial prayer is that the Father 'sent the Spirit of his Son into our hearts, crying, "*Abba!* Father!" '[16] Since our prayer sets forth our desires before God, it is again the Father, 'he who searches the hearts of men', who 'knows what is the mind of the Spirit, because the Spirit intercedes for the

690

saints according to the will of God.'[17] The prayer to our Father is inserted into the mysterious mission of the Son and of the Spirit.

III. The Prayer of the Church

2767 This indivisible gift of the Lord's words and of the Holy Spirit who gives life to them in the hearts of believers has been received and lived by the Church from the beginning. The first communities prayed the Lord's Prayer three times a day,[18] in place of the 'Eighteen Benedictions' customary in Jewish piety.

2768 According to the apostolic tradition, the Lord's Prayer is essentially rooted in liturgical prayer:

> [The Lord] teaches us to make prayer in common for all our brethren. For he did not say 'my Father' who art in heaven, but 'our' Father, offering petitions for the common Body.[19]

---

13 Cf. *Jn* 17:7.
14 Cf. *Mt* 6:7; 1 *Kings* 18:26–29.
15 *Jn* 6:63.
16 *Gal* 4:6.

17 *Rom* 8:27.
18 Cf. *Didache* 8, 3: SCh 248, 174.
19 St John Chrysostom, *Hom. in Mt* 19, 4: PG 57, 278.

In all the liturgical traditions, the Lord's Prayer is an integral part of the major hours of the Divine Office. In the three sacraments of Christian initiation its ecclesial character is especially in evidence.

2769 In *Baptism* and *Confirmation*, the handing on (*traditio*) of the Lord's Prayer signifies new birth into the divine life. Since Christian prayer is our speaking to God with the very word of God, those who are 'born anew ... through the living and abiding word of God'[20] learn to invoke their Father by the one Word he always hears. They can henceforth do so, for the seal of the Holy Spirit's anointing is indelibly placed on their hearts, ears, lips, indeed their whole filial being. This is why most of the patristic commentaries on the *Our Father* are addressed to catechumens and neophytes. When the Church prays the Lord's Prayer, it is always the people made up of the 'new-born' who pray and obtain mercy.[21]

1243

2770 In the *Eucharistic liturgy* the Lord's Prayer appears as the prayer of the whole Church and there reveals its full meaning and efficacy. Placed between the *anaphora* (the Eucharistic prayer) and the communion, the Lord's Prayer sums up on the one hand all the petitions and intercessions expressed in the movement of the *epiclesis* and, on the other, knocks at the door of the Banquet of the kingdom which sacramental communion anticipates.

1350

2771 In the Eucharist, the Lord's Prayer also reveals the *eschatological* character of its petitions. It is the proper prayer of 'the end-time', the time of salvation that began with the outpouring of the Holy Spirit and will be fulfilled with the Lord's return. The petitions addressed to our Father, as distinct from the prayers of the old covenant, rely on the mystery of salvation already accomplished, once for all, in Christ crucified and risen.

1403

2772 From this unshakeable faith springs forth the hope that sustains each of the seven petitions, which express the groanings of the present age, this time of patience and expectation during which 'it does not yet appear what we shall be.'[22] The Eucharist and the Lord's Prayer look eagerly for the Lord's return, 'until he comes.'[23]

1820

IN BRIEF

2773 *In response to his disciples' request 'Lord, teach us to pray' (Lk 11:1), Jesus entrusts them with the fundamental Christian prayer, the Our Father.*

---

20 *1 Pt* 1:23.
21 Cf. *1 Pt* 2:1–10.

22 *1 Jn* 3:2 ; cf. *Col* 3:4.
23 *1 Cor* 11:26.

2774 'The Lord's Prayer is truly the summary of the whole gospel,'[24] the 'most perfect of prayers.'[25] It is at the centre of the Scriptures.

2775 It is called 'The Lord's Prayer' because it comes to us from the Lord Jesus, the master and model of our prayer.

2776 The Lord's Prayer is the quintessential prayer of the Church. It is an integral part of the major hours of the Divine Office and of the sacraments of Christian initiation: Baptism, Confirmation and Eucharist. Integrated into the Eucharist it reveals the eschatological character of its petitions, hoping for the Lord, 'until he comes.' (1 Cor 11:26)

ARTICLE 2
'Our Father, Who Art in Heaven'

I. 'We Dare to Say'

2777 In the Roman liturgy, the Eucharistic assembly is invited to pray to our heavenly Father with filial boldness; the Eastern liturgies develop and use similar expressions: 'dare in all confidence', 'make us worthy of ...' From the burning bush Moses heard a voice saying to him, 'Do not come near; put off your shoes from your feet, for the place on which you are standing is holy ground.'[26] Only Jesus could cross that threshold of the divine holiness, for 'when he had made purification for sins', he brought us into the Father's presence: 'Here am I, and the children God has given me.'[27]

> Our awareness of our status as slaves would make us sink into the ground and our earthly condition would dissolve into dust, if the authority of our Father himself and the Spirit of his Son had not impelled us to this cry ... 'Abba, Father!' ... When would a mortal dare call God 'Father', if man's innermost being were not animated by power from on high?[28]

270

2778 This power of the Spirit who introduces us to the Lord's Prayer is expressed in the liturgies of East and of West by the beautiful, characteristically Christian expression: *parrhēsia*, straightforward simplicity, filial trust, joyous assurance, humble boldness, the certainty of being loved.[29]

2828

---

24 Tertullian, *De orat*.1:PL 1, 1251–1255.
25 St Thomas Aquinas, *STh* II–II, 83, 9.
26 *Ex* 3:5.
27 *Heb* 1:3, 2:13.
28 St Peter Chrysologus, *Sermo* 71, 3: PL 52, 401CD; cf. *Gal* 4:6.
29 Cf. *Eph* 3:12; *Heb* 3:6; 4:16; 10:19; 1 *Jn* 2:28; 3:21; 5:14.

II. 'Father!'

2779 Before we make our own this first exclamation of the Lord's Prayer, we must humbly cleanse our hearts of certain false images drawn 'from this world.' *Humility* makes us recognise that 'no one knows the Son except the Father, and no one knows the Father except the Son and anyone to whom the Son chooses to reveal him', that is, 'to little children.' [30] The *purification* of our hearts has to do with paternal or maternal images, stemming from our personal and cultural history, and influencing our relationship with God. God our Father transcends the categories of the created world. To impose our own ideas in this area 'upon him' would be to fabricate idols to adore or pull down. To pray to the Father is to enter into his mystery as he is and as the Son has revealed him to us.

239

> The expression God the Father had never been revealed to anyone. When Moses himself asked God who he was, he heard another name. The Father's name has been revealed to us in the Son, for the name 'Son' implies the new name 'Father.' [31]

2780 We can invoke God as 'Father' because *he is revealed to us* by his Son become man and because his Spirit makes him known to us. The personal relation of the Son to the Father is something that man cannot conceive of nor the angelic powers even dimly see: and yet, the Spirit of the Son grants a participation in that very relation to us who believe that Jesus is the Christ and that we are born of God.[32]

240

2781 When we pray to the Father, we are *in communion with him* and with his Son, Jesus Christ.[33] Then we know and recognise him with an ever new sense of wonder. The first phrase of the *Our Father* is a blessing of adoration before it is a supplication. For it is the glory of God that we should recognise him as 'Father', the true God. We give him thanks for having revealed his name to us, for the gift of believing in it, and for the indwelling of his Presence in us.

2665

2782 We can adore the Father because he has caused us to be re-born to his life by *adopting* us as his children in his only Son: by Baptism, he incorporates us into the Body of his Christ; through the anointing of his Spirit who flows from the head to the members, he makes us other 'Christs'.

1267

> God, indeed, who has predestined us to adoption as his sons, has conformed us to the glorious Body of Christ. So then you who have become sharers in Christ are appropriately called 'Christs'.[34]

---

30 *Mt* 11:25–27.   33 Cf. 1 *Jn* 1:3.
31 Tertullian, *De orat.* 3: PL 1, 1257A.   34 St Cyril of Jerusalem, *Catech.*
32 Cf. *Jn* 1:1; 1 *Jn* 5:1.   *myst.* 3, 1: PG 33, 1088A.

The new man, reborn and restored to his God by grace , says first of all, 'Father!' because he has now begun to be a son.[35]

1701

2783 Thus the Lord's Prayer *reveals us to ourselves* at the same time that it reveals the Father to us.[36]

O man, you did not dare to raise your face to heaven, you lowered your eyes to the earth, and suddenly you have received the grace of Christ: all your sins have been forgiven. From being a wicked servant you have become a good son ... Then raise your eyes to the Father who has begotten you through Baptism, to the Father who has redeemed you through his Son, and say: 'Our Father ...' But do not claim any privilege. He is the Father in a special way only of Christ, but he is the common Father of us all, because while he has begotten only Christ, he has created us. Then also say by his grace, 'Our Father', so that you may merit being his son.[37]

1428

2784 The free gift of adoption requires on our part continual conversion and *new life*. Praying to our Father should develop in us two fundamental dispositions:

First, *the desire to become like him*: though created in his image, we are restored to his likeness by grace; and we must respond to this grace.

1997

We must remember ... and know that when we call God 'our Father' we ought to behave as sons of God.[38]

You cannot call the God of all kindness your Father if you preserve a cruel and inhuman heart; for in this case you no longer have in you the marks of the heavenly Father's kindness.[39]

We must contemplate the beauty of the Father without ceasing and adorn our own souls accordingly.[40]

2562

2785 Second, *a humble and trusting heart* that enables us 'to turn and become like children':[41] for it is to 'little children' that the Father is revealed.[42]

[The prayer is accomplished] by the contemplation of God alone, and by the warmth of love, through which the soul, moulded and directed to love him, speaks very familiarly to God as to its own Father with special devotion.[43]

---

35 St Cyprian, *De Dom. orat.* 9: PL 4, 525A.

36 Cf. *GS* 22 § 1.

37 St Ambrose, *De sacr.* 5, 4, 19: PL 16:470.

38 St Cyprian, *De Dom. orat.* 11: PL 4:526B.

39 St John Chrysostom, *De orat Dom.* 3: PG 51, 44.

40 St Gregory of Nyssa, *De orat. dom.* 2: PG 44, 1148B.

41 *Mt* 18:3.

42 Cf. *Mt* 11:25.

43 St John Cassian, *Coll.* 9,18: PL 49, 788C.

Our Father: at this name love is aroused in us ... and the confidence of obtaining what we are about to ask ... What would he not give to his children who ask, since he has already granted them the gift of being his children? [44]

III. 'Our' Father

2786 'Our' Father refers to God. The adjective, as used by us, does not express possession, but an entirely new relationship with God.

443

2787 When we say 'our' Father, we recognise first that all his promises of love announced by the prophets are fulfilled in the *new and eternal covenant* in his Christ: we have become 'his' people and he is henceforth 'our' God. This new relationship is the purely gratuitous gift of belonging to each other: we are to respond to 'grace and truth' given us in Jesus Christ with love and faithfulness.[45]

782

2788 Since the Lord's Prayer is that of his people in the 'end-time', this 'our' also expresses the certitude of our hope in God's ultimate promise: in the new Jerusalem he will say to the victor, 'I will be his God and he shall be my son.'[46]

2789 When we pray to 'our' Father, we personally address the Father of our Lord Jesus Christ. By doing so we do not divide the Godhead, since the Father is its 'source and origin', but rather confess that the Son is eternally begotten by him and the Holy Spirit proceeds from him. We are not confusing the persons, for we confess that our communion is with the Father and his Son, Jesus Christ, in their one Holy Spirit. The *Holy Trinity* is consubstantial and indivisible. When we pray to the Father, we adore and glorify him together with the Son and the Holy Spirit.

245

253

2790 Grammatically, 'our' qualifies a reality common to more than one person. There is only one God, and he is recognised as Father by those who, through faith in his only Son, are reborn of him by water and the Spirit.[47] The *Church* is this new communion of God and men. United with the only Son, who has become 'the firstborn among many brethren', she is in communion with one and the same Father in one and the same Holy Spirit.[48] In praying 'our' Father, each of the baptised is praying in this communion: 'The company of those who believed were of one heart and soul.'[49]

787

2791 For this reason, in spite of the divisions among Christians, this prayer to 'our' Father remains our common patrimony and an ur-

821

---

44 St Augustine, *De serm. Dom. in monte* 2, 4, 16: PL 34, 1276.
45 *Jn* 1:17; cf. *Hos* 2:21–22; 6:1–6.
46 *Rev* 21:7.

47 Cf. 1 *Jn* 5:1; *Jn* 3:5.
48 *Rom* 8:29; cf. *Eph* 4:4–6.
49 *Acts* 4:32.

gent summons for all the baptised. In communion by faith in Christ and by Baptism, they ought to join in Jesus' prayer for the unity of his disciples.[50]

2792 Finally, if we pray the *Our Father* sincerely, we leave individualism behind, because the love that we receive frees us from it. The 'our' at the beginning of the Lord's Prayer, like the 'us' of the last four petitions, excludes no one. If we are to say it truthfully, our divisions and oppositions have to be overcome.[51]

2793 The baptised cannot pray to 'our' Father without bringing before him all those for whom he gave his beloved Son. God's love has no bounds, neither should our prayer.[52] Praying 'our' Father opens to us the dimensions of his love revealed in Christ: praying with and for all who do not yet know him, so that Christ may 'gather into one the children of God.' [53] God's care for all men and for the whole of creation has inspired all the great practitioners of prayer; it should extend our prayer to the full breadth of love whenever we dare to say 'our' Father.

604

IV. 'Who Art in Heaven'

2794 This biblical expression does not mean a place ('space'), but a way of being; it does not mean that God is distant, but majestic. Our Father is not 'elsewhere': he transcends everything we can conceive of his holiness. It is precisely because he is thrice-holy that he is so close to the humble and contrite heart.

326

> 'Our Father who art in heaven' is rightly understood to mean that God is in the hearts of the just, as in his holy temple. At the same time, it means that those who pray should desire the one they invoke to dwell in them.[54]

> 'Heaven' could also be those who bear the image of the heavenly world, and in whom God dwells and tarries.[55]

2795 The symbol of the heavens refers us back to the mystery of the covenant we are living when we pray to our Father. He is in heaven, his dwelling place; the Father's house is our homeland. Sin has exiled us from the land of the covenant,[56] but conversion of heart enables us to return to the Father, to heaven.[57] In Christ, then, heaven and earth are reconciled,[58] for the Son alone 'descended from heaven'

1024

---

50 Cf. *UR* 8; 22.
51 Cf. *Mt* 5:23–24; 6:14–15.
52 Cf. *NA* 5.
53 *Jn* 11:52.
54 St Augustine, *De serm. Dom. in monte* 2, 5, 18: PL 34, 1277.

55 St Cyril of Jerusalem, *Catech. myst.* 5:11: PG 33, 1117.
56 Cf. *Gen* 3.
57 *Jer* 3:19–4:1a; *Lk* 15:18, 21.
58 Cf. *Is* 45:8; *Ps* 85:12.

and causes us to ascend there with him, by his Cross, Resurrection and Ascension.[59]

2796 When the Church prays 'our Father who art in heaven', she is professing that we are the People of God, already seated 'with him in the heavenly places in Christ Jesus' and 'hidden with Christ in God';[60] yet at the same time, 'here indeed we groan, and long to put on our heavenly dwelling.'[61]

1003

> [Christians] are in the flesh, but do not live according to the flesh. They spend their lives on earth, but are citizens of heaven.[62]

IN BRIEF

2797 Simple and faithful trust, humble and joyous assurance are the proper dispositions for one who prays the Our Father.

2798 We can invoke God as 'Father' because the Son of God made man has revealed him to us. In this Son, through Baptism, we are incorporated and adopted as sons of God.

2799 The Lord's Prayer brings us into communion with the Father and with his Son, Jesus Christ. At the same time it reveals us to ourselves (cf. GS 22 § 1).

2800 Praying to our Father should develop in us the will to become like him, and foster in us a humble and trusting heart.

2801 When we say 'Our' Father, we are invoking the new covenant in Jesus Christ, communion with the Holy Trinity, and the divine love which spreads through the Church to encompass the world.

2802 'Who art in heaven' does not refer to a place but to God's majesty and his presence in the hearts of the just. Heaven, the Father's house, is the true homeland toward which we are heading and to which, already, we belong.

---

59 *Jn* 3:13; 12:32; 14:2–3; 16:28; 20:17;   61 *2 Cor* 5:2; cf. *Phil* 3:20; *Heb* 13:14.
    Eph 4:9–10; *Heb* 1:3; 2:13.   62 *Ad Diognetum* 5: PG 2, 1173.
60 *Eph* 2:6; *Col* 3:3.

ARTICLE 3
The Seven Petitions

2627

2803 After we have placed ourselves in the presence of God our Father to adore and to love and to bless him, the Spirit of adoption stirs up in our hearts seven petitions, seven blessings. The first three, more theologal, draw us toward the glory of the Father; the last four, as ways toward him, commend our wretchedness to his grace. 'Deep calls to deep.' [63]

2804 The first series of petitions carries us toward him, for his own sake: *thy* name, *thy* kingdom, *thy* will! It is characteristic of love to think first of the one whom we love. In none of the three petitions do we mention ourselves; the burning desire, even anguish, of the beloved Son for his Father's glory seizes us:[64] 'hallowed be thy name, thy kingdom come, thy will be done ...' These three supplications were already answered in the saving sacrifice of Christ, but they are henceforth directed in hope toward their final fulfilment, for God is not yet all in all.[65]

1105

2805 The second series of petitions unfolds with the same movement as certain Eucharistic epicleses: as an offering up of our expectations, that draws down upon itself the eyes of the Father of mercies. They go up from us and concern us from this very moment, in our present world: 'give *us* ... forgive *us* ... lead *us* not ... deliver *us* ...' The fourth and fifth petitions concern our life as such – to be fed and to be healed of sin; the last two concern our battle for the victory of life – that battle of prayer.

2656–2658

2806 By the three first petitions, we are strengthened in faith, filled with hope and set aflame by charity. Being creatures and still sinners, we have to petition for us, for that 'us' bound by the world and history, which we offer to the boundless love of God. For through the name of his Christ and the reign of his Holy Spirit our Father accomplishes his plan of salvation, for us and for the whole world.

2142–2159 ## I.   'Hallowed Be Thy Name'

2097

2807 The term 'to hallow' is to be understood here not primarily in its causative sense (only God hallows, makes holy), but above all in an evaluative sense: to recognise as holy, to treat in a holy way. And so, in adoration, this invocation is sometimes understood as praise and thanksgiving.[66] But this petition is here taught to us by Jesus as an optative: a petition, a desire and an expectation in which God and man are involved. Beginning with this first petition to our

---

63 *Ps* 42:7.
64 Cf. *Lk* 22:14 ; 12:50.

65 Cf. 1 *Cor* 15:28.
66 Cf. *Ps* 111:9; *Lk* 1:49.

Father, we are immersed in the innermost mystery of his Godhead and the drama of the salvation of our humanity. Asking the Father that his name be made holy draws us into his plan of loving kindness for the fullness of time, 'according to his purpose which he set forth in Christ', that we might 'be holy and blameless before him in love.'[67]

2808 In the decisive moments of his economy God reveals his name, but he does so by accomplishing his work. This work, then, is realised for us and in us only if his name is hallowed by us and in us.

203, 432

2809 The holiness of God is the inaccessible centre of his eternal mystery. What is revealed of it in creation and history, Scripture calls 'glory', the radiance of his majesty.[68] In making man in his image and likeness, God 'crowned him with glory and honour', but by sinning, man fell 'short of the glory of God.'[69] From that time on, God was to manifest his holiness by revealing and giving his name, in order to restore man to the image of his Creator.[70]

293

705

2810 In the promise to Abraham, and the oath that accompanied it,[71] God commits himself but without disclosing his name. He begins to reveal it to Moses and makes it known clearly before the eyes of the whole people when he saves them from the Egyptians: 'he has triumphed gloriously.'[72] From the covenant of Sinai onwards, this people is 'his own' and it is to be a 'holy (or 'consecrated': the same word is used for both in Hebrew) nation,'[73] because the name of God dwells in it.

63

2811 In spite of the holy Law that again and again their Holy God gives them – 'You shall be holy, for I the LORD your God am holy' – and although the Lord shows patience for the sake of his name, the people turn away from the Holy One of Israel and profane his name among the nations.[74] For this reason the just ones of the Old Covenant, the poor survivors returned from exile, and the prophets burned with passion for the name.

2143

2812 Finally, in Jesus the name of the Holy God is revealed and given to us, in the flesh, as Saviour, revealed by what he is, by his word, and by his sacrifice.[75] This is the heart of his priestly prayer: 'Holy Father ... for their sake I consecrate myself, that they also may be consecrated in truth.'[76] Because he 'sanctifies' his own name, Jesus reveals to us the name of the Father.[77] At the end of Christ's

434

---

67 *Eph* 1:9, 4.
68 Cf. *Ps* 8; *Is* 6:3.
69 *Ps* 8:5; *Rom* 3:23; cf. *Gen* 1:26..
70 *Col* 3:10.
71 Cf. *Heb* 6:13.
72 *Ex* 15:1; cf. 3:14.

73 Cf. *Ex* 19:5–6.
74 *Ezek* 20:9, 14, 22, 39; cf. *Lev* 19:2.
75 Cf. *Mt* 1:21; *Lk* 1:31; *Jn* 8:28; 17:8; 17:17–19.
76 *Jn* 17:11, 19.
77 Cf. *Ezek* 20:39; 36:20–21; *Jn* 17:6.

Passover, the Father gives him the name that is above all names: 'Jesus Christ is Lord, to the glory of God the Father.'[78]

2813 In the waters of Baptism, we have been 'washed ... sanctified ... justified in the name of the Lord Jesus Christ and in the Spirit of our God.'[79] Our Father calls us to holiness in the whole of our life, and since 'he is the source of [our] life in Christ Jesus, who became for us wisdom from God, and ... sanctification',[80] both his glory and our life depend on the hallowing of his name in us and by us. Such is the urgency of our first petition.

2013

> By whom is God hallowed, since he is the one who hallows? But since he said, 'You shall be holy to me; for I the LORD am holy', we seek and ask that we who were sanctified in Baptism may persevere in what we have begun to be. And we ask this daily, for we need sanctification daily, so that we who fail daily may cleanse away our sins by being sanctified continually ... We pray that this sanctification may remain in us.[81]

2814 The sanctification of his name among the nations depends inseparably on our *life* and our *prayer*:

2045

> We ask God to hallow his name, which by its own holiness saves and makes holy all creation ... It is this name that gives salvation to a lost world. But we ask that this name of God should be hallowed in us through our actions. For God's name is blessed when we live well, but is blasphemed when we live wickedly. As the Apostle says: 'The name of God is blasphemed among the Gentiles because of you.' We ask then that, just as the name of God is holy, so we may obtain his holiness in our souls.[82]

> When we say 'hallowed be thy name', we ask that it should be hallowed in us, who are in him; but also in others whom God's grace still awaits, that we may obey the precept that obliges us to pray for everyone, even our enemies. That is why we do not say expressly 'hallowed be thy name "in us" ', for we ask that it be so in all men.[83]

2815 This petition embodies all the others. Like the six petitions that follow, it is fulfilled by *the prayer of Christ*. Prayer to our Father is our prayer, if it is prayed *in the name* of Jesus.[84] In his priestly prayer, Jesus asks: 'Holy Father, protect in your name those whom you have given me.'[85]

2750

---

78 *Phil* 2:9-11.
79 1 *Cor* 6:11.
80 1 *Cor* 1:30 ; cf. 1 *Th* 4:7.
81 St Cyprian, *De Dom. orat.* 12: PL 4, 543–544; *Lev* 20:26.
82 St Peter Chrysologus, *Sermo* 71, 4: PL 52:402A; cf. *Rom* 2:24; *Ezek* 36: 20–22.
83 Tertullian, *De orat.* 3: PL 1:1257A.
84 Cf. *Jn* 14:13; 15:16; 16:24, 26.
85 *Jn* 17:11.

II. 'Thy Kingdom Come'

2816 In the New Testament, the word *basileia* can be translated by 'kingship' (abstract noun), 'kingdom' (concrete noun) or 'reign' (action noun). The Kingdom of God lies ahead of us. It is brought near in the Word incarnate, it is proclaimed throughout the whole Gospel, and it has come in Christ's death and Resurrection. The Kingdom of God has been coming since the Last Supper and, in the Eucharist, it is in our midst. The kingdom will come in glory when Christ hands it over to his Father:

541, 2632

560, 1107

> It may even be ... that the Kingdom of God means Christ himself, whom we daily desire to come, and whose coming we wish to be manifested quickly to us. For as he is our resurrection, since in him we rise, so he can also be understood as the Kingdom of God, for in him we shall reign.[86]

2817 This petition is '*Marana tha*', the cry of the Spirit and the Bride: 'Come, Lord Jesus'.

451

2632, 671

> Even if it had not been prescribed to pray for the coming of the kingdom, we would willingly have brought forth this speech, eager to embrace our hope. In indignation the souls of the martyrs under the altar cry out to the Lord: 'O Sovereign Lord, holy and true, how long before you judge and avenge our blood on those who dwell upon the earth?' For their retribution is ordained for the end of the world. Indeed, as soon as possible, Lord, may your kingdom come![87]

2818 In the Lord's Prayer, 'thy kingdom come' refers primarily to the final coming of the reign of God through Christ's return.[88] But, far from distracting the Church from her mission in this present world, this desire commits her to it all the more strongly. Since Pentecost, the coming of that Reign is the work of the Spirit of the Lord who 'complete[s] his work on earth and brings us the fullness of grace.'[89]

769

2819 'The kingdom of God [is] righteousness and peace and joy in the Holy Spirit.'[90] The end-time in which we live is the age of the outpouring of the Spirit. Ever since Pentecost, a decisive battle has been joined between 'the flesh' and the Spirit.[91]

2046

2516

> Only a pure soul can boldly say: 'Thy kingdom come.' One who has heard Paul say, 'Let not sin therefore reign in your mortal bodies', and

2519

---

86 St Cyprian, *De Dom. orat.* 13: PL 4, 544–545.
87 Tertullian, *De orat.* 5: PL 1, 1261–1262; cf. *Heb* 4:11; *Rev* 6:9; 22:20.
88 Cf. *Titus* 2:13.
89 *Roman Missal*, Eucharistic Prayer IV, 118.
90 *Rom* 14:17.
91 Cf. *Gal* 5:16–25.

has purified himself in action, thought and word will say to God: 'Thy kingdom come!'[92]

2820 By a discernment according to the Spirit, Christians have to distinguish between the growth of the Reign of God and the progress of the culture and society in which they are involved. This distinction is not a separation. Man's vocation to eternal life does not suppress, but actually reinforces, his duty to put into action in this world the energies and means received from the Creator to serve justice and peace.[93]

1049

2821 This petition is taken up and granted in the prayer *of* Jesus which is present and effective in the Eucharist; it bears its fruit in new life in keeping with the Beatitudes.[94]

2746

III. 'Thy Will Be Done on Earth as it is in Heaven'

851

2822 Our Father 'desires all men to be saved and to come to the knowledge of the truth.'[95] He 'is forbearing toward you, not wishing that any should perish.'[96] His commandment is 'that you love one another; even as I have loved you, that you also love one another.'[97] This commandment summarizes all the others, and expresses his entire will.

2196

59

2823 'He has made known to us the mystery of his will, according to his good pleasure that he set forth in Christ ... to gather up all things in him, things in heaven and things on earth. In Christ we have also obtained an inheritance, having been destined according to the purpose of him who accomplishes all things according to his counsel and will.'[98] We ask insistently for this loving plan to be fully realised on earth as it is already in heaven.

475

2824 In Christ, and through his human will, the will of the Father has been perfectly fulfilled once for all. Jesus said on entering into this world: 'Lo, I have come to do your will, O God.'[99] Only Jesus can say: 'I always do what is pleasing to him.'[100] In the prayer of his agony, he consents totally to this will: 'not my will, but your, be done.'[101] For this reason Jesus 'gave himself for our sins to deliver us from the present evil age, according to the will of our God and Father.'[102] 'And by that will we have been sanctified through the offering of the body of Jesus Christ once for all.'[103]

612

---

92 St Cyril of Jerusalem, *Catech. myst.* 5, 13: PG 33, 1120A; cf. *Rom* 6:12.
93 Cf. *GS* 22; 32; 39; 45; *EN* 31.
94 Cf. *Jn* 17:17-20; *Mt* 5:13-16; 6:24; 7:12-13.
95 1 *Tim* 2:3-4.
96 2 *Pt* 3:9; cf. *Mt* 18:14.
97 *Jn* 13:34; cf. 1 *Jn* 3; 4; *Lk* 10:25-37.
98 *Eph* 1:9-11.
99 *Heb* 10:7; *Ps* 40:7.
100 *Jn* 8:29.
101 *Lk* 22:42; cf. *Jn* 4:34; 5:30; 6:38.
102 *Gal* 1:4.
103 *Heb* 10:10.

2825 'Although he was a Son, [Jesus] learned obedience through what he suffered.'[104] How much more reason have we sinful creatures to learn obedience – we who in him have become children of adoption. We ask our Father to unite our will to his Son's, in order to fulfil his will, his plan of salvation for the life of the world. We are radically incapable of this, but united with Jesus and with the power of his Holy Spirit, we can surrender our will to him and decide to choose what his Son has always chosen: to do what is pleasing to the Father.[105]

615

> In committing ourselves to [Christ], we can become one spirit with him, and thereby accomplish his will, in such wise that it will be perfect on earth as it is in heaven.[106]

> Consider how [Jesus Christ] teaches us to be humble, by making us see that our virtue does not depend on our work alone but on grace from on high. He commands each of the faithful who prays to do so universally, for the whole world. For he did not say 'thy will be done in me or in us', but 'on earth', the whole earth, so that error may be banished from it, truth take root in it, all vice be destroyed on it, virtue flourish on it, and earth no longer differ from heaven.[107]

2826 By prayer we can discern 'what is the will of God' and obtain the endurance to do it.[108] Jesus teaches us that one enters the kingdom of heaven not by speaking words, but by doing 'the will of my Father in heaven.'[109]

2827 'If any one is a worshipper of God and does his will, God listens to him.'[110] Such is the power of the Church's prayer in the name of her Lord, above all in the Eucharist. Her prayer is also a communion of intercession with the all-holy Mother of God[111] and all the saints who have been pleasing to the Lord because they willed his will alone:

2611

> It would not be inconsistent with the truth to understand the words, 'Thy will be done on earth as it is in heaven', to mean: 'in the Church as in our Lord Jesus Christ himself'; or 'in the Bride who has been betrothed, just as in the Bridegroom who has accomplished the will of the Father.'[112]

796

IV. 'Give Us This Day Our Daily Bread'

2828 'Give us': The trust of children who look to their Father for everything is beautiful. 'He makes his sun rise on the evil and on the

2778

104 Heb 5:8.
105 Cf. Jn 8:29.
106 Origen, De orat. 26: PG 11, 501B.
107 St John Chrysostom, Hom. in Mt 19, 5: PG 57, 280.
108 Rom 12:2 ; cf. Eph 5:17; cf. Heb 10:36.
109 Mt 7:21.
110 Jn 9:31; cf. 1 Jn 5:14.
111 Cf. Lk 1:38, 49.
112 St Augustine, De serm. Dom. 2, 6, 24: PL 34, 1279.
113 Mt 5:45.

good, and sends rain on the just and on the unjust.'[113] He gives to all the living 'their food in due season.'[114] Jesus teaches us this petition, because it glorifies our Father by acknowledging how good he is, beyond all goodness.

2829 'Give us' also expresses the covenant. We are his and he is ours, for our sake. But this 'us' also recognises him as the Father of all men and we pray to him for them all, in solidarity with their needs and sufferings.

1939

2830 'Our bread': The Father who gives us life cannot not but give us the nourishment life requires – all appropriate goods and blessings, both material and spiritual. In the Sermon on the Mount, Jesus insists on the filial trust that co–operates with our Father's providence.[115] He is not inviting us to idleness,[116] but wants to relieve us from nagging worry and preoccupation. Such is the filial surrender of the children of God:

2633

> To those who seek the kingdom of God and his righteousness, he has promised to give all else besides. Since everything indeed belongs to God, he who possesses God wants for nothing, if he himself is not found wanting before God.[117]

227

2831 But the presence of those who hunger because they lack bread opens up another profound meaning of this petition. The drama of hunger in the world calls Christians who pray sincerely to exercise responsibility toward their brethren, both in their personal behaviour and in their solidarity with the human family. This petition of the Lord's Prayer cannot be isolated from the parables of the poor man Lazarus and of the Last Judgement.[118]

1038

2832 As leaven in the dough, the newness of the kingdom should make the earth 'rise' by the Spirit of Christ.[119] This must be shown by the establishment of justice in personal and social, economic and international relations, without ever forgetting that there are no just structures without people who want to be just.

1928

2833 'Our' bread is the 'one' loaf for the 'many'. In the Beatitudes 'poverty' is the virtue of sharing: it calls us to communicate and share both material and spiritual goods, not by coercion but out of love, so that the abundance of some may remedy the needs of others.[120]

2790
2546

---

114 *Ps* 104:27.
115 Cf. *Mt* 6:25–34.
116 Cf. *2 Th* 3:6–13.
117 St Cyprian, *De Dom. orat.* 21: PL 4, 534A.

118 Cf. *Lk* 16:19–31; *Mt* 25:31–46.
119 Cf. *AA* 5.
120 Cf. *2 Cor* 8:1–15.

2834 'Pray and work'.[121] 'Pray as if everything depended on God and work as if everything depended on you.'[122] Even when we have done our work, the food we receive is still a gift from our Father; it is good to ask him for it with thanksgiving, as Christian families do when saying grace at meals.   2428

2835 This petition, with the responsibility it involves, also applies to another hunger from which men are perishing: 'Man does not live by bread alone, but ... by every word that proceeds from the mouth of God',[123] that is, by the Word he speaks and the Spirit he breathes forth. Christians must make every effort 'to proclaim the good news to the poor.' There is a famine on earth, 'not a famine of bread, nor a thirst for water, but of hearing the words of the LORD.'[124] For this reason the specifically Christian sense of this fourth petition concerns the Bread of Life: The Word of God accepted in faith, the Body of Christ received in the Eucharist.[125]   2443   1384

2836 'This day' is also an expression of trust taught us by the Lord,[126] which we would never have presumed to invent. Since it refers above all to his Word and to the Body of his Son, this 'today' is not only that of our mortal time, but also the 'today' of God.   1165

> If you receive the bread each day, each day is today for you. If Christ is yours today, he rises for you every day. How can this be? 'You are my Son, today I have begotten you.' Therefore, 'today' is when Christ rises.[127]

2837 'Daily' (epiousios) occurs nowhere else in the New Testament. Taken in a temporal sense, this word is a pedagogical repetition of 'this day',[128] to confirm us in trust 'without reservation'. Taken in the qualitative sense, it signifies what is necessary for life, and more broadly every good thing sufficient for subsistence.[129] Taken literally (epi-ousios: 'super-essential'), it refers directly to the Bread of Life, the Body of Christ, the 'medicine of immortality', without which we have no life within us.[130] Finally in this connection, its heavenly meaning is evident: 'this day' is the Day of the Lord, the day of the Feast of the Kingdom, anticipated in the Eucharist that is already the foretaste of the Kingdom to come. For this reason it is fitting for the Eucharistic liturgy to be celebrated each day.   2659   2633   1405   1166   1389

> The Eucharist is our daily bread. The power belonging to this divine food makes it a bond of union. Its effect is then understood as unity, so

121 Cf. St Benedict, Regula, 20, 48.
122 Attributed to St Ignatius Loyola, cf. Joseph de Guibert, SJ, The Jesuits: Their Spiritual Doctrine and Practice, (Chicago: Loyola University Press, 1964), 148, n. 55.
123 Dt 8:3; Mt 4:4.
124 Am 8:11.
125 Cf. Jn 6:26–58.
126 Cf. Mt 6:34; Ex 16:19.
127 St Ambrose, De Sacr. 5, 4, 26: PL 16, 453A; cf. Ps 2:7.
128 Cf. Ex 16:19–21.
129 Cf. 1 Tim 6:8.
130 St Ignatius of Antioch, Ad Eph. 20, 2: PG 5, 661; Jn 6:53–56.

that, gathered into his Body and made members of him, we may become what we receive ... This also is our daily bread: the readings you hear each day in church and the hymns you hear and sing. All these are necessities for our pilgrimage.[131]

The Father in heaven urges us, as children of heaven, to ask for the bread of heaven. [Christ] himself is the bread who, sown in the Virgin, raised up in the flesh, kneaded in the Passion, baked in the oven of the tomb, reserved in churches, brought to altars, furnishes the faithful each day with food from heaven.[132]

V. 'And Forgive Us Our Trespasses, As We Forgive Those who Trespass Against Us'

2838 This petition is astonishing. If it consisted only of the first phrase, 'And forgive us our trespasses', it might have been included, implicitly, in the first three petitions of the Lord's Prayer, since Christ's sacrifice is 'that sins may be forgiven.' But, according to the second phrase, our petition will not be heard unless we have first met a strict requirement. Our petition looks to the future, but our response must come first, for the two parts are joined by the single word 'as'.

And forgive us our trespasses ...

2839 With bold confidence, we began praying to our Father. In begging him that his name be hallowed, we were in fact asking him that we ourselves might be always made more holy. But though we are clothed with the baptismal garment, we do not cease to sin, to turn away from God. Now, in this new petition, we return to him like the prodigal son and, like the tax collector, recognise that we are sinners before him.[133] Our petition begins with a 'confession' of our wretchedness and his mercy. Our hope is firm because, in his Son', 'we have redemption, the forgiveness of sins.'[134] We find the efficacious and undoubted sign of his forgiveness in the sacraments of his Church.[135]

2840 Now – and this is daunting – this outpouring of mercy cannot penetrate our hearts as long as we have not forgiven those who have trespassed against us. Love, like the Body of Christ, is indivisible; we cannot love the God we cannot see if we do not love the brother or sister we do see.[136] In refusing to forgive our brothers and sisters, our hearts are closed and their hardness makes them impervious to the Father's merciful love; but in confessing our sins, our hearts are opened to his grace.

1425

1933
2631

1425
1439

1422

1864

131 St Augustine, *Sermo* 57, 7: PL 38, 389.
132 St Peter Chrysologus, *Sermo* 67: PL 52, 392; cf. *Jn* 6:51.
133 Cf. *Lk* 15:11–32;18:13.
134 *Col* 1:14; *Eph* 1:7.
135 Cf. *Mt* 26:28; *Jn* 20:23.
136 Cf. 1 *Jn* 4:20

2841 This petition is so important that it is the only one to which the Lord returns and which he develops explicitly in the Sermon on the Mount.[137] This crucial requirement of the covenant mystery is impossible for man. But 'with God all things are possible.' [138]

... as we forgive those who trespass against us

2842 This 'as' is not unique in Jesus' teaching: 'You, therefore, must be perfect, *as* your heavenly Father is perfect'; 'Be merciful, even *as* your Father is merciful'; 'A new commandment I give to you, that you love one another, even *as* I have loved you, that you also love one another.' [139] It is impossible to keep the Lord's commandment by imitating the divine model from outside; there has to be a vital participation, coming from the depths of the heart, in the holiness and the mercy and the love of our God. Only the Spirit by whom we live can make 'ours' the same mind that was in Christ Jesus.[140] Then the unity of forgiveness becomes possible and we find ourselves 'forgiving one another, *as* God in Christ forgave' us.[141]

521

2843 Thus the Lord's words on forgiveness, the love that loves to the end,[142] become a living reality. The parable of the merciless servant, which crowns the Lord's teaching on ecclesial communion, ends with these words: 'So also my heavenly Father will do to every one of you, if you do not forgive your brother from your heart.' [143] It is there, in fact, 'in the depths of the *heart'*, that everything is bound and loosed. It is not in our power not to feel, or to forget, an offence; but the heart that offers itself to the Holy Spirit turns injury into compassion and purifies the memory in transforming the hurt into intercession.

368

2844 Christian prayer extends to the *forgiveness of enemies*,[144] transfiguring the disciple by configuring him to his Master. Forgiveness is a high-point of Christian prayer; only hearts attuned to God's compassion can receive the gift of prayer. Forgiveness also bears witness that, in our world, love is stronger than sin. The martyrs of yesterday and today bear this witness to Jesus. Forgiveness is the fundamental condition of the reconciliation of the children of God with their Father and of men with one another.[145]

2262

2845 There is no limit or measure to this essentially divine forgiveness,[146] whether one speaks of 'sins' as in *Luke* (11:4), or 'debts' as in *Matthew* (6:12). We are always debtors: 'Owe no–one anything,

1441

---

137 Cf. *Mt* 6:14-15; 5:23–24; *Mk* 11:25.
138 *Mt* 19:27.
139 *Mt* 5:48;*Lk* 6:36; *Jn* 13:34.
140 Cf. *Gal* 5:25; *Phil* 2:1, 5.
141 *Eph* 4:32.
142 Cf. *Jn* 13:1.

143 Cf. *Mt* 18:23–35.
144 Cf. *Mt* 5:43–44.
145 Cf. *2 Cor* 5:18–21; John Paul II, *DM* 14.
146 Cf. *Mt* 18:21–22; *Lk* 17:3–4.

except to love one another.'[147] The communion of the Holy Trinity is the source and criterion of truth in every relationship. It is lived out in prayer, above all in the Eucharist.[148]

> God does not accept the sacrifice of a sower of disunion, but commands that he depart from the altar so that he may first be reconciled with his brother. For God can be appeased only by prayers that make peace. To God, the better offering is peace, brotherly concord and a people made one in the unity of the Father, Son and Holy Spirit.[149]

VI. 'And Lead Us Not into Temptation'

2846 This petition goes to the root of the preceding one, for our sins result from our consenting to temptation; we therefore ask our Father not to 'lead' us into temptation. It is difficult to translate the Greek verb used by a single English word: the Greek means both 'do not allow us to enter into temptation', and 'do not let us yield to temptation.'[150] 'God cannot be tempted by evil and he himself tempts no one',[151] on the contrary, he wants to set us free from evil. We ask him not to allow us to take the way that leads to sin. We are engaged in the battle 'between flesh and spirit'; this petition implores the Spirit of discernment and strength.

164

2516

2847 The Holy Spirit makes us *discern* between trials, which are necessary for the growth of the inner man,[152] and temptation, which leads to sin and death.[153] We must also discern between being tempted, and consenting to temptation. Finally, discernment unmasks the lie of temptation, whose object appears to be good, a 'delight to the eyes' and desirable,[154] when in reality its fruit is death.

2284

> God does not want to impose the good, but wants free beings ... There is a certain usefulness to temptation. No–one but God knows what our soul has received from him, not even we ourselves. But temptation reveals it in order to teach us to know ourselves, and in this way we discover our evil inclinations and are obliged to give thanks for the goods that temptation has revealed to us.[155]

2848 'Lead us not into temptation' implies a *decision of the heart*: 'For where your treasure is, there will your heart be also ... No one can serve two masters.'[156] 'If we live by the Spirit, let us also walk by the Spirit.'[157] In this assent to the Holy Spirit the Father gives us strength. 'No testing has overtaken you that is not common to man.

1808

---

147 *Rom* 13:8.
148 Cf. *Mt* 5:23–24; 1 *Jn* 3:19–24.
149 St Cyprian, *De Dom. orat.* 23: PL 4, 535–536; cf. *Mt* 5:24.
150 Cf. *Mt* 26:41.
151 *Jas* 1:13.
152 Cf. *Lk.* 8:13–15; *Acts* 14:22;

Rom 5:3–5; 2 *Tim* 3:12.
153 Cf. *Jas* 1:14–15.
154 Cf. *Gen* 3:6.
155 Origen, *De orat.* 29: PG 11, 544CD.
156 *Mt* 6:21, 24.
157 *Gal* 5:25.

God is faithful, and he will not let you be tempted beyond your strength, but with the temptation will also provide the way of escape, so that you may be able to endure it.' [158]

2849   Such a battle and such a victory become possible only through prayer. It is by his prayer that Jesus vanquishes the tempter, both at the outset of his public mission and in the ultimate struggle of his agony[159] In this petition to our heavenly Father, Christ unites us to his battle and his agony. He urges us to *vigilance* of the heart in communion with his own. Vigilance is 'custody of the heart', and Jesus prayed for us to the Father: 'Keep them in your name.' [160] The Holy Spirit constantly seeks to awaken us to keep watch.[161] Finally, this petition takes on all its dramatic meaning in relation to the last temptation of our earthly battle; it asks for *final perseverance*. 'Lo, I am coming like a thief! Blessed is he who is awake.' [162]

540, 612

2612

162

VII. 'But Deliver Us from Evil'

2850   The last petition to our Father is also included in Jesus' prayer: 'I am not asking you to take them out of the world, but I ask you to protect them from the evil one.' [163] It touches each of us personally, but it is always 'we' who pray, in communion with the whole Church, for the deliverance of the whole human family. The Lord's Prayer continually opens us to the range of God's economy of salvation. Our interdependence in the drama of sin and death is turned into solidarity in the Body of Christ, the 'communion of saints.' [164]

309

2851   In this petition, evil is not an abstraction, but refers to a person, Satan, the Evil One, the angel who opposes God. The devil (*dia-bolos*) is the one who 'throws himself across' God's plan and his work of salvation accomplished in Christ.

391

2852   'A murderer from the beginning, ... a liar and the father of lies', Satan is 'the deceiver of the whole world.' [165] Through him sin and death entered the world and by his definitive defeat all creation will be 'freed from the corruption of sin and death.' [166] Now 'we know that anyone born of God does not sin, but He who was born of God keeps him, and the evil one does not touch him. We know that we are of God, and the whole world is in the power of the evil one.' [167]

---

158 1 *Cor* 10:13.
159 Cf. *Mt* 4:1–11; 26:36–44.
160 *Jn* 17:11; cf. *Mk* 13:9,23,33–37; 14:38; *Lk* 12:35–40.
161 Cf. 1 *Cor* 16:13; *Col* 4:2; 1 *Th* 5:6; 1 *Pt* 5:8.
162 *Rev* 16:15.

163 *Jn* 17:15.
164 Cf. *RP* 16.
165 *Jn* 8:44; *Rev* 12:9.
166 *Roman Missal*, Eucharistic Prayer IV, 125.
167 1 *Jn* 5:18–19.

The Lord who has taken away your sin and pardoned your faults also protects you and keeps you from the wiles of your adversary the devil, so that the enemy, who is accustomed to leading into sin, may not surprise you. One who entrusts himself to God does not dread the devil. 'If God is for us, who is against us?' [168]

677

490

972

2853 Victory over the 'prince of this world' [169] was won once for all at the Hour when Jesus freely gave himself up to death to give us his life. This is the judgement of this world, and the prince of this world is 'cast out.' [170] 'He pursued the woman' [171] but had no hold on her: the new Eve, 'full of grace' of the Holy Spirit, is preserved from sin and the corruption of death (the Immaculate Conception and the Assumption of the Most Holy Mother of God, Mary, ever virgin). 'Then the dragon was angry with the woman, and went off to make war on the rest of her offspring.' [172] Therefore the Spirit and the Church pray: 'Come, Lord Jesus,' [173] since his coming will deliver us from the Evil One.

2632

2854 When we ask to be delivered from the Evil One, we pray as well to be freed from all evils, present, past and future, of which he is the author or instigator. In this final petition, the Church brings before the Father all the distress of the world. Along with deliverance from the evils that overwhelm humanity, she implores the precious gift of peace and the grace of perseverance in expectation of Christ's return. By praying in this way, she anticipates in humility of faith the gathering together of everyone and everything in him who has 'the keys of Death and Hades', who 'is and who was and who is to come, the Almighty.' [174]

1041

Deliver us, Lord, we beseech you, from every evil and grant us peace in our day, so that aided by your mercy we might be ever free from sin and protected from all anxiety, as we await the blessed hope and the coming of our Saviour, Jesus Christ. [175]

ARTICLE 4
The Final Doxology

2760

2855 The final doxology, 'For the kingdom, the power and the glory are yours, now and forever,' takes up again, by inclusion, the first three petitions to our Father: the glorification of his name, the

---

168 St Ambrose, *De Sacr.* 5, 4, 30: PL 16, 454; cf. *Rom* 8:31.
169 *Jn* 14:30.
170 *Jn* 12:31; *Rev* 12:11.
171 *Rev* 12:13–16.
172 *Rev* 12:17.
173 *Rev* 22:17, 20.
174 *Rev* 1:8, 18; cf. *Rev* 1:4; *Eph* 1:10.
175 *Missale Romanum*, Embolism after the Lord's Prayer, 126: *Libera nos, quæsumus, Domine, ab omnibus malis, da propitius pacem in diebus nostris, ut, ope misericordiæ tuæ adiuti, et a peccato simus semper liberi, et ab omni perturbatione securi: expectantes beatam spem et adventum Salvatoris nostri Iesu Christi.*

coming of his reign and the power of his saving will. But these prayers are now proclaimed as adoration and thanksgiving, as in the liturgy of heaven.[176] The ruler of this world has mendaciously attributed to himself the three titles of kingship, power and glory.[177] Christ, the Lord, restores them to his Father and our Father, until he hands over the kingdom to him when the mystery of salvation will be brought to its completion and God will be all in all.[178]

2856 'Then, after the prayer is over you say "Amen", which means 1061–1065 "So be it", thus ratifying with our "Amen" what is contained in the prayer that God has taught us.' [179]

IN BRIEF

2857 In the Our Father, the object of the first three petitions is the glory of the Father: the sanctification of his name, the coming of the Kingdom and the fulfilment of his will. The four others present our wants to him: they ask that our lives be nourished, healed of sin and made victorious in the struggle of good over evil.

2858 By asking 'hallowed be thy name' we enter into God's plan, the sanctification of his name – revealed first to Moses and then in Jesus – by us and in us, in every nation and in each man.

2859 By the second petition, the Church looks first to Christ's return and the final coming of the Reign of God. It also prays for the growth of the Kingdom of God in the 'today' of our own lives.

2860 In the third petition, we ask our Father to unite our will to that of his Son, so as to fulfil his plan of salvation in the life of the world.

2861 In the fourth petition, by saying 'give us', we express in communion with our brethren our filial trust in our heavenly Father. 'Our daily bread' refers to the earthly nourishment necessary to everyone for subsistence, and also to the Bread of Life: the Word of God and the Body of Christ. It is received in God's 'today', as the indispensable, (super-)essential nourishment of the feast of the coming Kingdom anticipated in the Eucharist.

2862 The fifth petition begs God's mercy for our offences, mercy which can penetrate our hearts only if we have learned to forgive our enemies, with the example and help of Christ.

2863 When we say 'lead us not into temptation' we are asking God not to allow us to take the path that leads to sin. This petition implores the Spirit of discernment and strength; it requests the grace of vigilance and final perseverance.

2864 In the last petition, 'but deliver us from evil', Christians pray to God with the Church to show forth the victory, already won by Christ, over the 'ruler of this world', Satan, the angel personally opposed to God and to his plan of salvation.

2865 By the final 'Amen', we express our 'fiat' concerning the seven petitions: 'So be it'.

---

176 Cf. Rev 1:6; 4:11; 5:13.
177 Cf. Lk 4:5-6.
178 1 Cor 15:24–28.

179 St Cyril of Jerusalem, Catech. myst. 5, 18: PG 33, 1124; cf. Lk 1:38.

THE CREED

THE APOSTLES' CREED

I believe in God,
the Father almighty,
creator of heaven and earth.

I believe in Jesus Christ,
his only Son, our Lord.
He was conceived by the power
    of the Holy Spirit
and born of the Virgin Mary.
He suffered under Pontius Pilate,
was crucified, died, and was
    buried.
He descended to the dead.
On the third day he rose again.
He ascended into heaven
and is seated at the right hand
    of the Father.
He will come again
to judge the living and the dead.

I believe in the Holy Spirit,
the holy catholic Church,
the communion of saints,
the forgiveness of sins,
the resurrection of the body,
and the life everlasting.

Amen.

THE NICENE CREED

We believe in one God,
the Father, the Almighty,
maker of heaven and earth,
of all that is, seen and unseen.

We believe in one Lord, Jesus
    Christ,
the only Son of God
eternally begotten of the Father,
God from God, Light from Light,
true God from true God,
begotten, not made,
one in Being with the Father.
Through him all things were
    made.
For us men and for our salvation
he came down from heaven:
by the power of the Holy Spirit
he became incarnate of the Virgin
    Mary,
and became man.

For our sake he was crucified
    under Pontius Pilate;
he suffered, died, and was buried.
On the third day he rose again
in accordance with the Scriptures;
he ascended into heaven
and is seated at the right hand
    of the Father.
He will come again in glory
to judge the living and the dead,
and his kingdom will have no end.

We believe in the Holy Spirit,
the Lord, the giver of life,
who proceeds from the Father
    and the Son.
With the Father and the Son he is
    worshipped and glorified.
He has spoken through the
    Prophets.

We believe in one holy
catholic and apostolic Church.
We acknowledge one baptism
for the forgiveness of sins.
We look for the resurrection of the dead,
and the life of the world to come.
Amen.

THE TEN COMMANDMENTS

Exodus 20:2–17	Deuteronomy 5:6–21	A Traditional Catechetical Formula
I am the LORD your God, who brought you out of the land of Egypt, out of the house of bondage.	I am the LORD your God, who brought you out of the land of Egypt, out of the house of bondage.	1. I am the LORD your God:
You shall have no other gods before me. You shall not make for yourself a graven image, or any likeness of anything that is in heaven above, or that is in the earth beneath, or that is in the water under the earth; you shall not bow down to them or serve them; for I the LORD your God am a jealous God, visiting the iniquity of the fathers upon the children to the third and the fourth generation of those who hate me, but showing steadfast love to thousands of those who love me and keep my commandments.	You shall have no other gods before me ...	you shall not have strange Gods before me.
You shall not take the name of the LORD your God in vain; for the LORD will not hold him guiltless who takes his name in vain.	You shall not take the name of the LORD your God in vain: ...	2. You shall not take the name of the LORD your God in vain.

Remember the sabbath day, to keep it holy. Six days you shall labour, and do all your work; but the seventh day is a sabbath to the LORD your God; in it you shall not do any work, you, or your son, or your daughter, your manservant, or your maidservant, or your cattle, or the sojourner who is within your gates; for in six days the LORD made heaven and earth, the sea, and all that is in them, and rested the seventh day; therefore the LORD blessed the sabbath day and hallowed it.

Observe the sabbath day, to keep it holy ...

3. Remember to keep holy the Lord's Day.

Honour your father and your mother,
that your days may be long in the land which the LORD your God gives you.

Honour your father and your mother ...

4. Honour your father and your mother.

You shall not kill.

You shall not kill.

5. You shall not kill.

You shall not commit adultery.

Neither shall you commit adultery.

6. You shall not commit adultery.

You shall not steal.

Neither shall you steal.

7. You shall not steal.

You shall not bear false witness against your neighbour.

Neither shall you bear false witness against your neighbour.

8. You shall not bear false witness against your neighbour.

You shall not covet your neighbour's house; you shall not covet your neighbour's wife, or his manservant, or his maidservant, or his ox, or his ass, or anything that is your neighbour's.

Neither shall you covet your neighbour's wife ...

9. You shall not covet your neighbour's wife.

You shall not desire... anything that is your neighbour's.

10. You shall not covet your neighbour's goods.

ABBREVIATIONS

AA	*Apostolicam actuositatem*	LG	*Lumen gentium*
AAS	Acta Apostolicae Sedis	LH	Liturgy of the Hours
AF	Lightfoot *Apostolic Fathers*	LXX	Septuagint
AG	*Ad gentes*	MC	*Marialis cultus*
CA	*Centesimus annus*	MD	*Mulieris dignitatem*
CCEO	Corpus Canonum Ecclesiarum	MF	*Mysterium fidei*
	Orientalium	MM	*Mater et magistra*
CChr	Corpus christianorum	NA	*Nostra aetate*
CCL	Corpus Christianorum, series latina	NCCB	National Conference of Catholic
CD	*Christus Dominus*		Bishops (USA)
CDF	Congregation for the Doctrine of	ND	Neuner–Dupuis, *The Christian*
	the Faith		*Faith in the Doctrinal Documents of*
CELAM	Latin American Episcopal Council		*the Catholic Church*
CIC	Codex Iuris Canonici (1983)	OC	Rite of Confirmation
CL	*Christifideles laici*	OCF	Order of Christian Funerals
COD	Conciliorum oecumenicorum	OCM	*Ordo celebrandi matrimonium*
	decreta	OCV	*Ordo consecrationis virginum*
CPG	*Credo of the People of God*	OE	*Orientalium ecclesiarum*
CSEL	Corpus scriptorum ecclesiasticorum	OP	*Ordo paenitentiae*
	latinorum	OR	Office of Readings
CT	*CATECHESI tradendi*	OT	*Optatam totius*
DeV	*Dominum et Vivificanum*	PC	*Perfectae caritatis*
DH	*Dignitatis humanae*	PG	Migne, *Patrologia graeca*
DM	*Dives in misericordia*	PL	Migne, *Patrologia latina*
DS	Denzinger-Schönmetzer,	PLS	Migne, *Patrologia latina*
	Enchiridion Symbolorum (1965)		Supplement
DV	*Dei Verbum*	PO	*Presbyterorum ordinis*
EN	*Evangelii nuntiandi*	PP	*Populorum progressio*
EP	Eucharistic Prayer	PT	*Pacem in terris*
FC	*Familiaris consortio*	RBC	Rite of Baptism of Children
GCD	*General Catechetical Directory*	RCIA	Rite of Christian Initiation of
GE	*Gravissimum educationis*		Adults
GILH	General Introduction to the	RH	*Redemptor hominis*
	Liturgy of the Hours	RMat	*Redemptoris Mater*
GIRM	General Instruction of the Roman	RMiss	*Redemptoris missio*
	Missal	RP	*Reconciliatio et paenitentia*
GS	*Gaudium et spes*	SC	*Sacrosanctum concilium*
HV	*Humanae vitae*	SCG	Summa contra gentiles
ICEL	International Commission on	SCh	Sources chrétiennes
	English in the Liturgy	SRS	*Sollicutdo rei socialis*
IM	*Inter mirifica*	STh	Summa theologiae
JB	Jerusalem Bible	UR	*Unitatis redintegratio*
LE	*Laborem exercens*		

INDEX OF CITATIONS

Sacred Scripture

13:33	2606
13:48	2640
17:27	2566
20:36	2636
21:5	2636

Romans

2:24	2814
3:23	2809
5:3–5	2734, 2847
5:5	2658
6:5	2565
6:12	2819
8:15	2777
8:16	2639
8:22	2630
8:23–24	2630
8:26–39	2739
8:26–27	2634
8:26	2559, 2630, 2736
8:27	2736, 2766
8:29	2790
8:31	2852
8:32	2572
8:34	2634
10:1	2632, 2636
10:12–13	2739
10:13	2666
12:2	2826
12:14	2636
13:8	2845
14:17	2819
15:5–6	2627
15:13	2627, 2657
15:30	2629
16:25-27	2641

1 Corinthians

6:11	2813
8:6	2639
10:13	2848
11:26	2772, 2776
12:3	2670, 2681
15:24–28	2855
15:28	2804
16:13	2849

2 Corinthians

1	2627
1:3–7	2627
4:6	2583
5:2	2796
5:18–21	2844
8:1–15	2833
9:14	2636
13:13	2627

Galatians

1:4	2824
2:20	2666
4:6	2766
5:16–25	2744, 2819
5:25	2842 2848

Ephesians

1:3–14	2627, 2641
1:4	2807
1:7	2839
1:9–11	2823
1:9	2603, 2807
1:10	2748
1:16–23	2632
2:6	2796
3:12	2778
3:16–17	2714
3:18–21	2565
4:4–6	2790
4:9–10	2795
4:32	2842
5:14	2641
5:17	2826
5:19	2641
5:20	2633, 2742
6:18–20	2636
6:18	2742
6:23–24	2627

Philippians

1:3–4	2636
1:9–11	2632
2:1	2842
2:4	2635
2:5	2842
2:6–11	2641, 2667
2:9-11	2812
3:20	2796
4:6-7	2633

Colossians

1:3–6	2632
1:3	2636
1:14	2839
1:15-20	2641
3:3	2796
3:4	2772
3:10	2809
3:16–17	2633
3:16	2641
4:2	2638, 2849
4:3–4	2632, 2636
4:12	2629, 2632

1 Thessalonians

4:7	2813
5:6	2849
5:17–18	2633
5:17	2757
5:18	2638, 2648
5:25	2636

2 Thessalonians

1:11	2636
3:6-13	2830

1 Timothy

2:1	2636
2:3–4	2822
2:5–8	2634
2:5	2574
3:16	2641
6:8	2837
6:15–16	2641

2 Timothy

3:12	2847

Titus

2:13	2764, 2818

Hebrews

1:3	2777, 2795
2:12	2602
2:13	2777, 2795
2:15	2602
3:6	2778
4:15	2602
4:16	2778
5:7–9	2606
5:7	2741
5:8	2825
6:13	2810
7:25	2634, 2741
9:24	2741
10:5–7	2568
10:7	2824
10:10	2824
10:19	2778
10:36	2826
11:17	2572
11:19	2572
12:1	2683
13:14	2796

James

1:5–8	2633, 2737
1:13	2846
1:14–15	2847
1:17	2642
4:1–10	2737
4:2–3	2737
4:4	2737
4:5	2737
5:16	2737
5:16b–18	2582

1 Peter

1	2627
1:3–9	2627
1:23	2769
2:1–10	2769

2 Peter

3:9	2822

1 John

1:3	2781
1:7-2:2	2631
2:1	2634
2:28	2778
3	2822
3:2	2772
3:19–24	2845
3:21	2778
3:22	2631
4	2822
4:20	2840
5:1	2780, 2790
5:14	2778, 2827
5:18–19	2852

Jude		4:11	2855	16:15,	2849
24–25	2641	5:9–14	2642	18:24	2642
		5:13	2855	19:1-8	2642
Revelation		6:10	2642, 2817	21:3	2676
1:4	2854	7:10-12	2642	21:7	2788
1:6	2855	12:9	2852	22:17	2853
1:8	2854	12:11	2853	22:20	2853
1:18	2854	12:13–16	2853		
4:8–11	2642	12:17	2853		

Ecumenical Councils

(Cited by DS numbers, except for Vatican II)

VATICAN II (1962-1965)

Unitatis redintegratio
(21 November 1964)
22 — 2791

Perfectae caritatis
(28 October 1965)
2 — 2684
7 — 2691

Nostra aetate
(28 October 1965)
5 — 2793

Dei Verbum
(18 November 1965)
2 — 2587
8 — 2650, 2651
10 — 2663
25 — 2653

Apostolicam actuositatem
(18 November1965)
5 — 2832

Gaudium et spes
(7 December 1965)
22 — 2820
22, 1 — 2783, 2734
32 — 2820
39 — 2820
45 — 2820

Pontifical Documents

PAUL VI (1963–1978)
Ap. Exh. *Evangelii nuntiandi*
(8 December 1975)
31 — 2820

JOHN PAUL II (1978–)
Ap. Exh. *Catechesi tradendae*
(16 October 1979)
54 — 2688
55 — 2688

Ap. Exh. *Reconciliatio et Paenitentia*
(2 December 1984)
16 — 2850

Liturgy

LATIN RITE
Roman Missal
Eucharistic Prayer
I (Roman Canon)
IV — 2818, 2852

Embolism to the Lord's Prayer
126 — 2760, 2854

Sequence of Pentecost — 2671

Liturgy of the Hours
General Introduction
7 — 2616
9 — 2655
100–109 — 2586

Prayers
'Ave Maria' — 2676, 2677
'Veni sancte Spiritus' — 2671

EASTERN RITES
Byzantine Liturgy
Troparia
of Vespers, pentectost — 2671

Ecclesiastical Writers

ANONYMOUS AUTHORS
Constitutiones Apostolorum
7, 24, 1 — PG 1, 1016 — 2760

Didache XII Apostolorum
8, 2 — SCh 248, 174 — 2760
8, 3 — SCh 248, 174 — 2767

Epistula ad Diognetum
5, 5 — PG 2, 1173 — 2796

Alphonsus de Liguori, St (1696–1787)
Del gran mezzo della preghiera — 2741

Ambrose, St (339–397)
De officiis ministrorum
1, 88 — PL 16 (1880), 50A — 2653

De sacramentis
5, 19 — PL 16 (1880), 470 — 2783
5, 26 — PL 16 (1880), 472 — 2836
5, 30 — PL 16 (1880), 472 — 2852

Enarrationes in Psalmos
1, 9 — PL 14, 968 *LH, OR,*
week 10, Saturday — 2589

SUBJECT INDEX

Prefatory Note to Index

The main entry words are printed in bold type as are references to definitions or exact descriptions (for example, **Abraham**). References to 'In Brief' texts are printed in italics (for example, *Adoration*: *2696*). The sub headings that follow main entries provide additional information about the same or closely related topics (for example: **Abraham**: faith of Abraham: 2676). Cross references with 'see' or 'see also' supply information about relevant main entry words. The primary objective in constructing this index was to provide the most comprehensive survey possible of the contents, not the most complete listing of all references to a given subject.

Abraham:
faith of Abraham: 2676
prayer of Abraham: 2570–72, 2592, 2635
promise to Abraham: 2810
fulfillment of the promises: 2619

Acedia: [spiritual sloth]
as temptation in prayer: 2733

Adoration:
and blessing: 2781
of the Blessed Sacrament: 2691, *2696*

Altar: 2570

Blessing:
in God's plan of salvation: *2645*

Catechesis:
task: 2688

Church liturgy:
examination of forms of prayer by the
    Magisterium: 2663

Doxology: 2639–49, 2760, 2855
see also: Prayer, forms of

Eucharist:
sacrificial character:
    as sacrifice of praise: 2643

Family:
importance of family prayer: 2685

God:
actions with respect to man:
    adopts men as children: 2782–85
    calls man: 2567
God the Holy One:
    as mystery of his divinity: 2807
    God's holiness and glory: 2809
    in the life and prayer of the Christian: 2814
    in the revelation of the Old
        Testament: 2810–11
    in the revelation of Jesus: 2812

Hail Mary: 2676–78

Heart of Jesus, adoration of: 2669

Holiness; sanctity; saints:
saints:
    as companions in prayer: 2683–2684

Holy Spirit:
acts: in all mankind:
    master and source of prayer: 2652
Humility:
and prayer: 2559, 2628, 2631, 2706, 2713

Israel; Israelites:
Jacob as ancestor of the twelve tribes of
    Israel: 2573
see also: Prayer

Jesus Christ:
prayer of Jesus:
    as model for the prayer of disciples: 2601
    as prayer of the Son of the Father: 2599
    before important salvation
        events: 2600, 2602
    high priestly prayer: 2746-51
    important prayers of Jesus: 2603-6
    Jesus hears prayers: 2616
    Jesus teaches to pray: 2607-15
    Our Father: *2759*

Jesus Prayer: 2616, 2667–68

Lectio divina: 2708

Love:
interpretation and place:
    as source of prayer: 2658
see also Charity

Man:
search for God:
    God calls man first: 2567
    man always in search of God: 2566

Mary:
prayer of Mary: 2617–19

Meditation: 2705–8

Our Father:
eschatological character: 2771
importance: 2761–64, 2774
in the sacraments of initiation: 2769
in the Eucharistic celebration: 2770
'Lord's Prayer': 2765–66, *2773*, *2775*
prayer of the Church: 2767–68, 2776
seven petitions: 2803–54, 2857–65

Perfection: see Holiness

Praise: see Doxology; Prayer, forms of

Prayer:
and ordained ministers: 2686, 2695
as always possible: 2743
as vital necessity: 2744
bound up in the history of man:
    between the fall and restoration
        of man: 2568
    conversation at the burning bush: 2575
    in creation: 2569
    in Judaism: 2577, 2579, 2586
    in the Old Covenant: 2568–89, 2592–97
    prayer of Jesus: 2598–2616, 2620
    prayer of Mary 2617–19, 2622
    prayer of the Church: 2623–25
Christian prayer: 2564–65
    as cooperation with God's
        providence: 2738
    as man's answer to God's call: 2560–62
    as precondition for obeying God's
        commandments: 2098
    different traditions: 2650–51, 2684
    meaning of the word 'Amen': 1061–65
    prayer and life as
        inseparable: 2725, 2745, 2752
    relationship to God in: 2786–88, 2592
    special place of Jesus in
        possible only in Christ's name: 2664
efficacy: 2738–41
family prayer: 2685, 2694
for the dying: 2299
God's thirst and human thirst: 2560
heaven as God's 'place': 2794–96
humility as foundation: 2559
importance of catechesis: 2688
in communion with Mary: 2673–79, 2682
in the community of believers: 2790–93
Jesus teaches how to pray:
    by means of his own prayer: 2607, 2621
    conversion of heart: 2608
    in order to do the will of the Father: 2611
    in three important parables: 2613
    prayer in faith: 2609
    prayer in filial boldness: 2610
    prayer in the Holy Spirit: 2615, 2661
    to ask in his name: 2614
    vigilance in prayer: 2612, 2730
meaning and importance: 2590
objections to: 2726–27
saints as masters of prayer: 2683–84, 2692
sources of: 2662
    every day: 2659–60
    faith: 2098, 2656
    Holy Spirit: 2652
    hope: 2098, 2657
    liturgy of the Church: 2655
    love: 2098, 2658
    Word of God: 2653–54
to Jesus: 2616, 2665–69, 2681
to the Father: 2680, 2779–85, 2788, 2792,
    2797–2802
to the Holy Spirit: 2670–72
trust in prayer: 2777–78
'without ceasing': 2742
Prayer, difficulties in: 2728
inner dryness: 2731

distractions: 2729
doubts: 2735–37, 2756

Prayer, forms of:
adoration: 2628
blessing: 2626–27
ecclesial forms of prayer: 2625
great range of forms of Christian
    prayer: 2663, 2644, 2684, 2693
petition: 2629
    for the 'coming of the Kingdom of
        God': 2816, 2646
    in every need and occasion: 2633
    in Holy Scripture: 2630
    intercession: 2634–36, 2647
    praise of God: 2639–43, 2649
        as foundational movement of
            Christian prayer: 2626
        the 'hallowing' of God's
            name: 2807–15
    request for daily bread: 2828–37
    request for deliverance from evil: 2850–54
    request for forgiveness: 2631, 2838–41
    request for love of neighbor and
        of enemies: 2842
    request for the spirit of discernment and
        power: 2846
    thanksgiving: 2637–38
    see also: Doxology
see also: Prayer, ways of

Prayer, life of: 2697

Prayer, places of: 2691, 2696

Prayer, temptations at:
acedia: 2733, 2755
lack of faith: 2732, 2755

Prayer, ways of:
contemplative prayer: 2709–19, 2721, 2724
meditation: 2705-8, 2721, 2723
vocal prayer: 2700-2704, 2721–22

Prayer groups: 2689

Psalms:
as prayer of the People of God: 2586
as school of prayer: 2587
importance for daily prayer: 2589
in the liturgy of the Old Covenant: 2588
Psalms as book of the Old Testament: 2585
'Psalms of David': 2579

Rosary: 2708

Saints: see Holiness

Scripture, Sacred:
significance:
    as source of prayer: 2653–54

Sloth: see acedia

Spirit: see Holy Spirit

Theologal Life: 2607, 2803

Way of the Cross: 2669

Women:
as image of the Church: 2853